FAITH LESSONS

ON THE
early
CHURCH

CONQUERING THE GATES OF HELL

LEADER'S GUIDE

Also Available from Ray Vander Laan

Video and Group Resources

Faith Lessons on the Death and Resurrection of the Messiah
Faith Lessons on the Life and Ministry of the Messiah
Faith Lessons on the Promised Land
Faith Lessons on the Prophets and Kings of Israel

Book and Audiocassette

Echoes of His Presence

CD-Rom

Jesus: An Interactive Journey

FAITH LESSONS

ON THE early CHURCH

CONQUERING THE GATES OF HELL

LEADER'S GUIDE

Ray Vander Laan

with
Stephen and Amanda Sorenson

ZondervanPublishingHouse
Grand Rapids, Michigan

A Division of HarperCollinsPublishers

Faith Lessons on the Early Church Leader's Guide
Copyright © 2000 by Ray Vander Laan

Requests for information should be addressed to:

ZondervanPublishingHouse
Grand Rapids, Michigan 49530

ISBN 0-310-67968-0

Interior design by Sherri Hoffman

Printed in the United States of America

06 07 /❖VG / 10 9 8 7 6

contents

Introduction

Because God speaks to us through the Scriptures, studying them is a rewarding experience. The inspired human authors of the Bible, as well as those to whom the words were originally given, were Jews living in the Middle East. God's words and actions spoke to them with such power, clarity, and purpose that they wrote them down and carefully preserved them as an authoritative body of literature.

God's use of human servants in revealing Himself resulted in writings that clearly bear the stamp of time and place. The message of the Scriptures is, of course, eternal and unchanging—but the circumstances and conditions of the people of the Bible are unique to their times. Consequently, we most clearly understand God's truth when we know the cultural context within which He spoke and acted and the perception of the people with whom He communicated. This does not mean that God's revelation is unclear if we don't know the cultural context. Rather, by learning how to think and approach life as Abraham, Moses, Ruth, Esther, and Paul did, modern Christians will deepen their appreciation of God's Word. To fully apply the message of the Bible to our lives, we must enter the world of the Bible and familiarize ourselves with its culture.

That is the purpose of this study. The events and characters of the Bible will be presented in their original settings. Although the videos offer the latest archaeological research, this series is not intended to be a definitive cultural and geographical study of the lands of the Bible. No original scientific discoveries are revealed here. The purpose of this study is to help us better understand God's revealed mission for our lives by enabling us to hear and see His words in their original context.

understanding the world of the Bible

More than 3,800 years ago, God spoke to His servant Abraham: "Go, walk through the length and breadth of the land, for I am giving it to you" (Genesis 13:17). From the outset, God's choice of a Hebrew nomad to begin His plan of salvation (that is still unfolding) was linked to the selection of a specific land where His redemptive work would begin. The nature of God's covenant relationship with His people demanded a place where their faith could be exercised and displayed to all nations so that the world would know of *Yahweh*, the true and faithful God. God showed the same care in preparing a land for His chosen people as He did in preparing a people to live in that land. For us to fully understand God's plan and purpose for His people, we must first understand the nature of the place He selected for them.

In the Old Testament, God promised to protect and provide for the Hebrews. He began by giving them Canaan—a beautiful, fertile land where He would shower His blessings upon them. To possess this land, however, the Israelites had to live obediently before God. The Hebrew Scriptures repeatedly link Israel's obedience to God to the nation's continued possession of Canaan, just as they link its disobedience to the punishment of exile (Leviticus 18:24–28). When the Israelites were exiled from the Promised Land (2 Kings 18:11), they did not experience God's blessings. Only when they possessed the land did they know the fullness of God's promises.

By New Testament times, the Jewish people had been removed from the Promised Land by the Babylonians due to Israel's failure to live obediently before God (Jeremiah 25:4–11). The exile lasted seventy years, but its impact upon God's people was astounding. New patterns of worship developed, and scribes and experts in God's law shaped the new commitment to be faithful to Him. The prophets predicted the appearance of a Messiah like King David who would revive the kingdom of the Hebrew people.

But the Promised Land had become home to many other groups of people whose religious practices, moral values, and lifestyles conflicted with those of the Jews. Living as God's witnesses took on added difficulty as Greek, Roman, and Samaritan worldviews mingled with that of the Israelites. The Promised Land was divided between kings and governors, usually under the authority of one foreign empire or another. But the mission of God's people did not change. They were still to live so that *the world may know that our God is the true God*. And the land continued to provide them opportunity to encounter the world that desperately needed to know this reality.

The Promised Land was the arena within which God's people would serve Him faithfully as the world watched. The land God chose for His people was on the crossroads of the world. A major trade route, the Via Maris, ran through it. God intended for the Israelites to take control of the cities along this route and thereby exert influence on the nations around them. Through their righteous living, the Hebrews would reveal the one true God, *Yahweh*, to the world. They failed to accomplish this mission, however, because of their unfaithfulness.

The Jewish Gospel in a Greek World

From the beginning, God's plan was to reclaim His world. The Jewish people of the Bible had made God known to many of the nations of the world as people from those nations traveled through Israel. The Assyrian dispersion and the Babylonian exile spread God-fearing Jewish people around the known world. Many of them returned to Jerusalem for the yearly feasts that God had commanded. God had prepared carefully and well for the next stage in His great plan of salvation: His people must now live *so that the world may know* in all the world—not just in one small place.

If the arena had changed, the mission had not. The people of God would reveal Him to people in places such as Rome, Athens, and the cities of Roman provinces such as Syria and Macedonia. The most pagan of all provinces, Asia Minor, would become a stronghold for the followers of God and the Messiah Jesus. They would serve Him while the nations of the world watched and listened.

The triumph of the Christian faith is nowhere more striking or unexpected than in the Roman Province of Asia Minor. Known for immorality in lifestyle and in religious practice, this region became Christian within 150 years of Jesus' ministry in Israel. The early missionary, Paul (Shaul in Hebrew), spent a great deal of time here and wrote several letters to the followers of Jesus in this province. Peter wrote his letters to the believers here, and John wrote Revelation (and his letters) to the churches of this province. The effectiveness of the early believers is amazing and raises a host of questions with great implications for our world today. How did Jesus prepare His followers for such a mission? What empowered them? What kind of commitments did they have to make to their mission? What did they do that had such an impact on the people of Asia? Some answers to these questions become clear when we study the biblical stories in the context in which they occurred.

pliny

One of the most important sources of information about life in Asia Minor at the time of the early church comes from a Roman governor named Pliny. His letters, written to the emperor Trajan (A.D. 98–117), are a fascinating description of the relationship between the early believers and the pagan Gentiles in the province of Asia Minor. Pliny's work provides helpful insights for understanding the stories and teachings of Scripture. In addition, Pliny provides many insights into the view of the new faith held by the people of his time who were not Christians.

Trajan had appointed Pliny to bring order to the area of Pontus (in Asia Minor) because of riots and unrest due to local corruption. Pliny proceeded to ban all social, political, and religious organizations, which created great suffering for the Christians because they were not considered one of the legal religions. Pliny noted that the "superstition" (Christianity) had spread throughout the province and left ancient temples deserted.

Pliny made it clear that being a Christian was a capital offense, and many were accused and charged. Pliny offered them several chances to renounce their faith, and then they were executed. In one letter to Trajan, he asked what should be done to those who renounced their faith. Were they still criminals for their actions while they were members of the sect, or was their rejection of Jesus sufficient? Trajan replied by making adherence to Christianity a capital offense, although the believers were not to be sought out.

our purpose

Biblical writers assumed that their readers were familiar with Middle Eastern geography. Today, unfortunately, many Christians do not have even a basic geographical knowledge of the region. This study is designed to help solve that problem. We will be studying the people and events of the Bible in their geographical and historical contexts. Once we know the who, what, and where of a Bible story, we will be able to understand the why. By deepening our understanding of God's Word, we will be able to strengthen our relationships with Him.

Western Christianity tends to spiritualize the faith of the people of the Bible. Modern Christians do not always do justice to God's desire that His people live faithfully for Him in specific places, influencing the cultures around them by their words and actions. Instead of seeing the places to which God called His people as crossroads from which to influence the world, we focus on the glorious destination to which we are traveling as we ignore the world around us. We are focused on the destination, not the journey. We have unconsciously separated our walk with God from our responsibility to the world in which He has placed us.

In one sense, our earthly experience is simply preparation for an eternity in the new "Promised Land." Preoccupation with this idea, however, distorts the mission God has set for us. That mission is the same one He gave to the Israelites: to live obediently *within* the world so that through us, *the world may know that our God is the one true God.*

How to use This guide

This Leader's Guide is divided into five sessions approximately fifty-five minutes in length. Each session corresponds to a videotaped presentation by Ray Vander Laan.

For each session, *the leader* will need:

- Leader's Guide
- Bible
- Video player, monitor, stand, extension cord, etc.
- Videotape

Note: For some sessions, the leader may also want to use an overhead projector, chalkboard, or marker board.

For each session, *the participant* will need:

- Participant's Guide
- Bible
- Pen or pencil

Directions to the leader are enclosed in the shaded boxes and are not meant to be spoken.

Each session is divided into six main parts: **Before You Lead, Introduction, Video Presentation, Group Discovery, Faith Lesson,** and **Closing Prayer**. A brief explanation of each part follows.

1. Before You Lead

Synopsis

This material is presented for the leader's information. It summarizes the material presented in each of the videos.

Key Points of This Lesson

Highlights the key points you'll want to emphasize.

Session Outline

Provides an overview of the content and activities to be covered throughout the session.

Materials

The materials listed above are critical for both the leader and each participant. Additional materials (optional) are listed when appropriate.

2. Introduction

Welcome
Welcomes participants to the session.

What's to Come
A brief summary you may choose to use as you begin the session.

Questions to Think About
Designed to help everyone begin thinking about the theme or topics that will be covered. A corresponding page is included in the Participant's Guide.

3. Video Presentation

This is the time during which you and the participants will watch the video and write down appropriate notes. Key themes have been indicated.

4. Group Discovery

In this section, you'll guide participants in thinking through materials and themes related to the video you've just seen. You may want to read the material word for word, or simply highlight key words and phrases. Feel free to amplify various points with your own material or illustrations.

The Leader's Guide includes a copy of the corresponding pages in the Participant's Guide. Space is also provided in which to write additional planning notes. Having the Participant's Guide pages in front of you allows you to view the pages the participants are seeing as you talk without having to hold two books at the same time. It also lets you know where the participants are in their book when someone asks you a question.

Video Highlights
Use these questions and suggested responses with the entire group. This will guide participants in verbally responding to key points/themes covered in the video.

Small Group Bible Discovery
At this time, if your group has more than seven participants you will break the group into small groups (three to five people) and assign each group a topic. (If you have more groups than topics, assign some topics to more than one group.) Participants will use their Bibles and write down suggested responses to the questions. If time allows, representatives of the small groups can share key ideas their groups discussed.

Quite often supplementary material—called *Data File, Profile,* etc.—has been inserted near the topics. This material complements the themes but is not required reading to complete the session. Suggest that the participants read and study the supplementary material on their own.

5. Faith Lesson

Time for Reflection

At this time, participants will read selected Scripture passages and think about questions that encourage them to apply what they've just discovered to their own lives.

Action Points

At this time, you'll summarize key points (provided for you) with the entire group and encourage participants to act on what they have learned.

6. Closing Prayer

Close the session with the material or prayer provided.

Before the First Session

- Watch the video session.
- Obtain the necessary Participant's Guides for all participants.
- Make sure you have the necessary equipment.

Tips for Leading and Promoting Group Discussion

1. Allow group members to participate at their own comfort level. Everyone need not answer every question.
2. Ask questions with interest and warmth and then listen carefully to individual responses. Remember: it is important for participants to think through the questions and ideas presented. The *process* is more important than specific *answers*, which is why *suggested responses* are provided.
3. Be flexible. Reword questions if necessary. Choose to spend more time on a topic. Add or delete questions to accommodate the needs of your group members—and your time frame.
4. Suggest that participants, during the coming week, do the Small Group Bible Discovery topics that their individual small groups may not have had the opportunity to do.
5. Allow for (and expect) differences of opinion and experience.
6. Gently guide all participants into discussion. Do not allow any person(s) to monopolize discussion.
7. Should a heated discussion begin on a theological topic, suggest that the participants involved continue their discussion after the session is over.
8. Do not be afraid of silence. Allow people time to think—don't panic. Sometimes ten seconds of silence seems like an eternity. Remember, some of this material requires time to process—so allow people time to digest a question and *then* respond.

everything to lose, nothing to gain

before you lead

Synopsis

After the death and ascension of Jesus the Messiah, His disciples boldly proclaimed His message to the world. They didn't stop at the borders of Galilee—or even Israel—the lands with which they were familiar and in which they felt comfortable. They pressed on to the far reaches of the Roman Empire—even to the extremely pagan province of Asia Minor (present-day Turkey).

Asia Minor was the most pagan and immoral province of the entire Roman Empire. It wasn't a place that God-fearing, Jewish people would choose to go to on their own. So what gave Jesus' disciples the passion to endure hardship and persecution in order to share His message in such a place? What inspired them to go to a place where they had nothing to gain for their efforts—indeed, where they had everything to lose, even life itself? What had Jesus done to prepare them to live out His teachings in daily life and to minister so boldly?

In this video, Ray Vander Laan takes us to three places—Korazin, Caesarea Philippi, and the Mount of Olives—where Jesus chose, trained, and taught His disciples. Each location gives us insight into the answers to these questions.

Like other Jewish rabbis of His day, Jesus had disciples (*talmidim* in Hebrew) who earnestly desired not only to know what He knew but to act as He acted and to take on the godly character He possessed. Whereas most *talmidim* sought out the rabbis they wished to follow, Jesus personally *chose* His disciples. Interestingly, Jesus chose nearly all of His disciples from Galilee, a very religious area where the town of Korazin is located.

Fully intending for His disciples to pass along His teachings to others, Jesus came to fulfill the Torah. This meant that Jesus applied the Torah to daily life and demonstrated how God wanted His people to live. He constantly interpreted the Torah for the disciples so that they could learn to obey it as God intended. Whereas most people in Asia Minor did not make a connection between their religion and how they lived, the disciples discovered that God's truths were deeply connected to daily life. The faith that Jesus taught required a passionate commitment to action, a commitment to be like Him.

When Jesus taught, He used word pictures and literal, concrete illustrations of familiar objects that made it easier for His listeners to understand His message. Later, as the disciples journeyed into Asia Minor to carry out His mandate, they used the same teaching method. They also, in imitation of Jesus' relationship with them, established nurturing communities of believers that would support, encourage, and, when necessary, correct one another as they sought to live out their faith. This community of believers, the early church, stood in stark contrast to the Greek disciples who were trained to stand alone and to be self-sufficient in their own knowledge.

Ray then takes us to the pagan shrines at Caesarea Philippi, a city located on a plateau at the foot of Mount Hermon, Israel's highest mountain. Jesus deliberately took His disciples the thirty miles from Galilee to this stronghold of pagan worship. Here, a river of spring-fed water rushed forth from a deep cave at the base of a rock cliff more than one hundred feet high. The place was called "the gates of Hades" because the cave was believed to be the entrance to the underworld (Hades), through which the fertility god Pan would pass on his way to and from the underworld.

In this seemingly strange location, Jesus asked, "Who am I?" to which Peter replied, "You are the Messiah, the Son of the Living God." What a key lesson this was! The disciples, who would soon go into places where people worshiped Roman emperors and dozens of pagan gods, needed to know with certainty that Jesus was the *living* Messiah.

Near this site Jesus also issued the statement, "On this rock I will build my church." The rock cliff near "the gates of Hades" represented everything that was disgusting and wrong with the world. Yet Jesus wanted His disciples to build His church on top of that rock—to replace the pagan values with His values. Furthermore, He said, "the gates of Hades will not prevail against it." He wanted His disciples to know that nothing they'd encounter in Asia Minor or anywhere else could stand against His power. In His name, the disciples could attack even the power of Hell itself!

Jesus then challenged His disciples and the pagan crowd to deny themselves and follow Him. He challenged them to give up trying to gain meaning and purpose, significance and value, from life and to give their lives to others as He would do. He challenged them to never be ashamed of Him or His words. Jesus' boldness in teaching them while they were surrounded by pagan worshipers in Caesarea Philippi must have given the disciples courage when they later spoke to kings, priests, and hostile Gentiles in palaces, temples, theaters, and arenas.

After His resurrection, Jesus spent an additional forty days teaching His followers. But one lesson remained. Jesus took them to the Mount of Olives where He commanded them to be His witnesses "in Jerusalem, Judea, Samaria, and to the ends of the earth." Then, He raised His hands to bless them and ascended to heaven while they watched.

Perhaps He left them in this way because the Roman emperors' claims to divinity would soon erupt into widespread emperor worship. Witnesses would claim to have seen the emperors ascending into heaven. But Jesus' disciples had actually witnessed the divine Son of God—the King of Kings and Lord of Lords—ascending to heaven to sit at His Father's right hand. They could travel the world and confidently declare that Jesus, indeed, was the Son of God. Their message would result in numerous confrontations with peoples and powers that would lead many disciples to their deaths. Yet their message fanned a passionate faith that changed the world.

Key Points of This Lesson

1. *As a rabbi, Jesus prepared His chosen disciples—His talmidim—to carry on His message after He was gone.* He lived in community with them, interpreting and modeling the Torah so that they would know how to live God's way. He taught them about His faith, which is a passionate commitment to act in accordance with what they believed.

2. *Shortly before going to Jerusalem for the last time, Jesus took His disciples to Caesarea Philippi, a pagan worship center. Here, His disciples realized anew that He was the Messiah, the Son of the living God.* He also assured them that His church would triumph—even over the gates of Hades (hell). How important this truth would become when the disciples faced personal suffering, even martyrdom, because of their commitment to Him.

3. *As eyewitnesses of His ascension, the disciples were empowered to boldly proclaim the message of Jesus to their world.* For His last teaching, Jesus took His disciples to the Mount of Olives and reminded them that they were His witnesses to the world. Then, before their eyes, He ascended into heaven. This dramatic scene inspired them to go out and tell everyone about the living Messiah who will one day return to claim His own.

Session Outline (55 minutes)

I. Introduction (4 minutes)
Welcome
What's to Come
Questions to Think About

II. Show Video "Follow Me" (31 minutes)

III. Group Discovery (15 minutes)
Video Highlights
Small Group Bible Discovery

IV. Faith Lesson (4 minutes)
Time for Reflection
Action Points

V. Closing Prayer (1 minute)

Materials

No additional materials are needed for this session; however, you may want to use a marker board, chalkboard, or overhead projector to record participants' responses to **Questions to Think About**. Please view the video prior to leading the session so you are familiar with its main points.

everything to lose, nothing to gain

introduction

4 minutes

Welcome

> Assemble the participants together. Welcome them to session one of *Faith Lessons on the Early Church.*

What's to Come

In this session, we'll learn about how Jesus, the rabbi, prepared His chosen disciples for their future ministry in the unbelievably pagan cities of Asia Minor, which today we know as Turkey. We'll visit the ruins of the synagogue of Korazin in Galilee, the region in which Jesus did most of His teaching. Next, we'll visit Caesarea Philippi, a city famous for its pagan worship. Here, Jesus taught His disciples—and some startled pagan worshipers—key lessons concerning His identity as the living Messiah and the church's power to triumph over evil. Finally, we will visit the Mount of Olives, where Jesus concluded His disciples' teaching by ascending into heaven while they watched. We will see how these events empowered Jesus' disciples to go out and change their world.

Questions to Think About

> *Participant's Guide page 13.*
>
> Ask each question and solicit a few responses from group members. You may want to write these responses on a marker board, chalkboard, or overhead projector so that participants may view them as the session progresses.

1. Take a minute to list what you find to be the most difficult places or situations in which to minister in the world around you.

   Suggested Responses: These will vary. Encourage participants to think of a variety of specific places and situations.

SESSION ONE

everything to lose, nothing to gain

questions to think about

1. Take a minute to list what you find to be the most difficult places or situations in which to minister in the world around you.

2. What factors make it difficult to share your faith in these places or situations?

PLANNING NOTES:

✏ 2.   What factors make it difficult to share your faith in these places or situations?

Suggested Responses: These will vary, and they will overlap. Your list may be similar to the obstacles Jesus' disciples faced when they went into Asia Minor.

Let's keep these ideas in mind as we view the video.

video presentation

31 minutes

Participant's Guide page 14.

On page 14 of your Participant's Guide, you will find space in which to take notes on key points as we watch this video.

Leader's Video Observations

Galilee—Jesus the Rabbi Builds a Community of Followers

Caesarea Philippi—Jesus Asks the All-Important Question

The Mount of Olives—Jesus Delivers His Final Message

everything to lose, nothing to gain

questions to think about

1. Take a minute to list what you find to be the most difficult places or situations in which to minister in the world around you.

2. What factors make it difficult to share your faith in these places or situations?

---

video notes

Galilee—Jesus the Rabbi Builds a Community of Followers

Caesarea Philippi—Jesus Asks the All-Important Question

The Mount of Olives—Jesus Delivers His Final Message

PLANNING NOTES:

group discovery
15 minutes

If your group has seven or more members, use the **Video Highlights** with the entire group (5 minutes), then break into small groups of three to five to discuss the **Small Group Bible Discovery** (10 minutes).

If your group has fewer than seven members, begin with the **Video Highlights** (5 minutes), then do one or more of the topics found in the **Small Group Bible Discovery** as a group (10 minutes).

Video Highlights (5 minutes)

Here you'll ask one or more of the following questions that directly relate to the video the participants have just seen.

1. Note the region of Asia Minor on the map of the Roman Empire below. Which characteristics of this area made it a seemingly unlikely place for Jewish disciples from Galilee to evangelize?

    Suggested Responses: It was very pagan, the easiest access required a voyage across the eastern Mediterranean Sea, etc.

2. In what specific ways did Jesus the rabbi, through His personal relationship with His disciples, prepare them for their future ministry?

    Suggested Responses: He personally chose each of them, showing that He believed in them; He came to interpret the Torah and to demonstrate how to

The Roman Empire

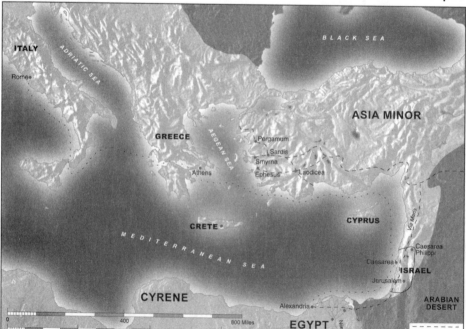

video нighlights

1. Note the region of Asia Minor on the map of the Roman Empire on page 16. Which characteristics of this area made it a seemingly unlikely place for Jewish disciples from Galilee to evangelize?

2. In what specific ways did Jesus the rabbi, through His personal relationship with His disciples, prepare them for their future ministry?

3. Why was it so important for the disciples—as Peter did in Caesarea Philippi—to affirm who Jesus was?

4. Why was it so important for the disciples to actually see Jesus ascend to heaven?

16   Faith Lessons on the Early Church

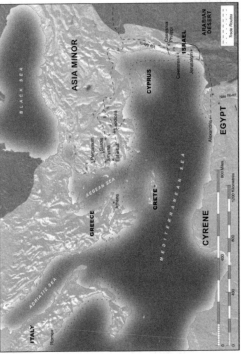

The Roman Empire

apply it correctly to daily life; He used word pictures and concrete illustrations in His teaching; He taught them how to cooperate together, in community; He demonstrated that faith requires a passionate commitment to action; etc.

✏ 3. Why was it so important for the disciples—as Peter did in Caesarea Philippi—to affirm who Jesus was?

Suggested Responses: They needed to know, without doubt, that He was truly the living God, not just another false god; they needed to know that He had power over evil; etc.

✏ 4. Why was it so important for the disciples to actually see Jesus ascend to heaven?

Suggested Responses: Being eyewitnesses of His ascension helped give them the boldness and courage to confront the worship of false gods and Roman emperors, etc.

Small Group Bible Discovery (10 minutes)

Participant's Guide pages 17.

During this time, a group with fewer than seven participants will stay together. A group larger than seven participants will break into small groups. Assign each group one of the following topics. If you have more than five small groups, assign some topics to more than one group.

Let's break into groups of three to five—people sitting near you—and study some of the Bible passages and truths mentioned in the video.

Turn to pages 17–33 in your Participant's Guide. There you'll find a list of five topics. You'll have ten minutes to read and discuss the topic I'll assign to you.

Assign each group a topic.

I'll signal you when one minute is left.

Topic A: Jesus the Rabbi

After learning the construction trade with Joseph, His earthly father, Jesus became a teacher—a rabbi. During Jesus' time, the term *rabbi* did not refer to a specific office or occupation. Rather, it was a term of respect, meaning "great one" or "my master." The students of a rabbi—*talmidim*—were passionately devoted to him. They watched and noted everything he said and did so that they could do the same. As the rabbi lived and interpreted the Torah, his disciples sought to imitate him. Their overriding passion was to become like him. Eventually, they also would become teachers, passing on what they'd learned to their *talmidim*.

video highlights

1. Note the region of Asia Minor on the map of the Roman Empire on page 16. Which characteristics of this area made it a seemingly unlikely place for Jewish disciples from Galilee to evangelize?

2. In what specific ways did Jesus the rabbi, through His personal relationship with His disciples, prepare them for their future ministry?

3. Why was it so important for the disciples—as Peter did in Caesarea Philippi—to affirm who Jesus was?

4. Why was it so important for the disciples to actually see Jesus ascend to heaven?

small Group Bible Discovery

Topic A: Jesus the Rabbi

After learning the construction trade with Joseph, His earthly father, Jesus became a teacher—a rabbi. During Jesus' time, the term *rabbi* did not refer to a specific office or occupation. Rather, it was a term of respect, meaning "great one" or "my master." The students of a rabbi—*talmidim*—were passionately devoted to him. They watched and noted everything he said and did so that they could do the same. As the rabbi lived and interpreted the Torah, his disciples sought to imitate him. Their overriding passion was to become like him. Eventually, they also would become teachers, passing on what they'd learned to their *talmidim*.

Galilee of Jesus' Ministry

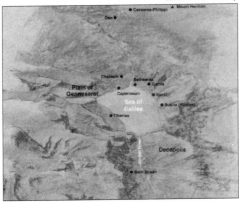

PLANNING NOTES:

Galilee of Jesus' Ministry

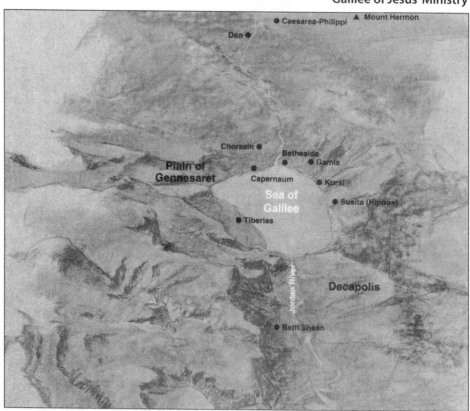

1. In which area of Israel did Jesus conduct His ministry and perform most of His miracles? What were the people there like? (See Matthew 4:13–16; 11:20–24.)

   Suggested Responses: Jesus chose to conduct most of His ministry near the Sea of Galilee in Korazin, Bethsaida, and Capernaum, which was an area populated primarily by religious Jews.

   Note: For at least the first fifty years after Jesus' ascension, the Christian community remained strongest in Galilee. Perhaps the Galileans took Jesus' rebuke in Matthew 11:21–24 to heart.

2. Each rabbi encouraged his disciples to take on the "yoke of Torah," to commit to obeying Torah as the rabbi interpreted and taught it. How did Jesus describe His "yoke," and how did it compare to the "yoke" of some other rabbis? (See Matthew 11:28–30; 23:1–4.)

   Suggested Responses: Speaking to people who were overburdened and weary from trying to understand many difficult interpretations of the Torah, Jesus described His yoke as "easy" and "light," providing "rest" for their souls. Jesus practiced what He preached and did not, as some rabbis did, burden His disciples with heavy loads that He was unwilling to carry.

small Group bible Discovery

Topic A: Jesus the Rabbi

After learning the construction trade with Joseph, His earthly father, Jesus became a teacher—a rabbi. During Jesus' time, the term *rabbi* did not refer to a specific office or occupation. Rather, it was a term of respect, meaning "great one" or "my master." The students of a rabbi—*talmidim*—were passionately devoted to him. They watched and noted everything he said and did so that they could do the same. As the rabbi lived and interpreted the Torah, his disciples sought to imitate him. Their overriding passion was to become like him. Eventually, they also would become teachers, passing on what they'd learned to their *talmidim*.

Galilee of Jesus' Ministry

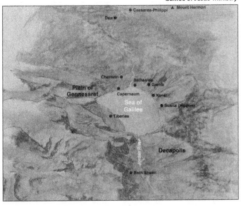

18   Faith Lessons on the Early Church

1. In which area of Israel did Jesus conduct His ministry and perform most of His miracles? What were the people there like? (See Matthew 4:13–16; 11:20–24.)

2. Each rabbi encouraged his disciples to take on the "yoke of Torah," to commit to obeying Torah as the rabbi interpreted and taught it. How did Jesus describe His "yoke," and how did it compare to the "yoke" of some other rabbis? (See Matthew 11:28–30; 23:1–4.)

3. To be a *talmid* meant far more than to learn what the rabbi knew. What do the following verses reveal about what Jesus wanted His disciples to be and do—how He wanted them to live out their faith in daily life?

Reference	What It Meant to Be Like the Rabbi
Matthew 28:16–20	
Mark 1:16–20	
Mark 3:13–19	

3. To be a *talmid* meant far more than to learn what the rabbi knew. What do the following verses reveal about what Jesus wanted His disciples to be and do—how He wanted them to live out their faith in daily life?

Reference	What It Meant to Be Like the Rabbi
Matthew 28:16–20	*to make disciples—people who would obey all of Jesus' teaching*
Mark 1:16–20	*to "follow" Him*
Mark 3:13–19	*to "be with Him," to be sent out to preach, and to combat evil*
Luke 6:40	*to be like Him—their teacher*
Luke 9:1–6	*to exercise His authority and do what He did—go from village to village preaching, healing, and defeating evil*
Luke 14:26–27	*to make following Him their major focus*
John 8:31	*to obey His teaching*
John 13:13–17	*to imitate His actions*

THE TRUTH OF THE MATTER

The "Yoke" of the Kingdom of Heaven

Many Christians today recognize that salvation is a gift from God and so place little emphasis on "keeping the law" of the Bible. It is true that Jesus did away with "law keeping" by obeying the law completely and by offering salvation through grace to everyone who trusts in Him. Yet it is also true that Jesus did not suggest that obedience to the Word of God was any less important because of His completed work. In fact, He commanded His followers to "go and make disciples . . . teaching them to *obey everything* I have commanded you" (Matthew 28:19–20, italics added).

If we are to be like Jesus—to be His disciples—we must desire to be like Him in all ways, which includes obeying Him as He obeys His Father. Just as obedience was vital to the first-century disciples who went to pagan regions and proclaimed God's way to live, obedience is vital to us today. If we are to impact our world for God, we must have the same commitment to the lifestyle God demands and Jesus exemplified.

18   Faith Lessons on the Early Church

1. In which area of Israel did Jesus conduct His ministry and perform most of His miracles? What were the people there like? (See Matthew 4:13–16; 11:20–24.)

2. Each rabbi encouraged his disciples to take on the "yoke of Torah," to commit to obeying Torah as the rabbi interpreted and taught it. How did Jesus describe His "yoke," and how did it compare to the "yoke" of some other rabbis? (See Matthew 11:28–30; 23:1–4.)

3. To be a *talmid* meant far more than to learn what the rabbi knew. What do the following verses reveal about what Jesus wanted His disciples to be and do—how He wanted them to live out their faith in daily life?

Reference	What It Meant to Be Like the Rabbi
Matthew 28:16–20	
Mark 1:16–20	
Mark 3:13–19	

Session One: Everything to Lose, Nothing to Gain   19

Luke 6:40	
Luke 9:1–6	
Luke 14:26–27	
John 8:31	
John 13:13–17	

THE TRUTH OF THE MATTER

The "Yoke" of the Kingdom of Heaven

Many Christians today recognize that salvation is a gift from God and so place little emphasis on "keeping the law" of the Bible. It is true that Jesus did away with "law keeping" by obeying the law completely and by offering salvation through grace to everyone who trusts in Him. Yet it is also true that Jesus did not suggest that obedience to the Word of God was any less important because of His completed work. In fact, He commanded His followers to "go and make disciples . . . teaching them to *obey everything* I have commanded you" (Matthew 28:19–20, italics added).

If we are to be like Jesus—to be His disciples—we must desire to be like Him in all ways, which includes obeying Him as He obeys His Father. Just as obedience was vital to the first-century disciples who went to pagan regions and proclaimed God's way to live, obedience is vital to us today. If we are to impact our world for God, we must have the same commitment to the lifestyle God demands and Jesus exemplified.

PROFILE OF A MASTER

Jesus the Master Teacher

The great teachers (rabbis) during Jesus' day used a technique that was later called *remez*. In their teaching, they would use part of a Scripture passage in a discussion, assuming that their audience's knowledge of the Bible would allow them to deduce for themselves the fuller meaning of the teaching. Apparently Jesus, who possessed a brilliant understanding of Scripture and strong teaching skills, used this method often.

For example, when the children shouted "Hosanna" to Him in the temple and the chief priests and teachers of the law became indignant (Matthew 21:15), Jesus responded by quoting Psalm 8:2:"From the lips of children and infants you have ordained praise." The religious leaders' anger at Jesus can be better understood when we realize that the next phrase in the psalm reveals why children and infants offer praise—because the enemies of God would be silenced. The religious leaders realized that Jesus was implying that they were God's enemies.

Jesus used this teaching method again when speaking to Zacchaeus."For the Son of Man came to seek and to save what was lost," Jesus said (Luke 19:10). The background to this statement is probably Ezekiel 34. God, angry with Israel's leaders for scattering and harming His flock, stated that He would become the shepherd and would seek the lost ones and save them. Based on this, the people of Jesus' day understood that the Messiah to come would "seek and save" the lost. By using this phrase, knowing that His listeners knew the Scripture, Jesus communicated several things. To the people, He communicated,"I am the Messiah and also God."To the religious leaders, whose influence kept Zacchaeus out of the crowd, He said,"You have scattered and harmed God's flock."To Zacchaeus, He said,"You are one of God's lost sheep, and He still loves you."

Jesus best fit the type of rabbi believed to have *s'mikhah,* the authority to make new interpretations of the Torah. Whereas most teachers of the law could only teach accepted interpretations, teachers with authority could make new interpretations and pass legal judgments. Crowds were amazed because Jesus taught with authority (Matthew 7:28–29), and some people questioned His authority (Matthew 21:23–27).

PROFILE OF A MASTER

Jesus the Master Teacher

The great teachers (rabbis) during Jesus' day used a technique that was later called *remez*. In their teaching, they would use part of a Scripture passage in a discussion, assuming that their audience's knowledge of the Bible would allow them to deduce for themselves the fuller meaning of the teaching. Apparently Jesus, who possessed a brilliant understanding of Scripture and strong teaching skills, used this method often.

For example, when the children shouted "Hosanna" to Him in the temple and the chief priests and teachers of the law became indignant (Matthew 21:15), Jesus responded by quoting Psalm 8:2: "From the lips of children and infants you have ordained praise." The religious leaders' anger at Jesus can be better understood when we realize that the next phrase in the psalm reveals why children and infants offer praise—because the enemies of God would be silenced. The religious leaders realized that Jesus was implying that they were God's enemies.

Jesus used this teaching method again when speaking to Zacchaeus. "For the Son of Man came to seek and to save what was lost," Jesus said (Luke 19:10). The background to this statement is probably Ezekiel 34. God, angry with Israel's leaders for scattering and harming His flock, stated that He would become the shepherd and would seek the lost ones and save them. Based on this, the people of Jesus' day understood that the Messiah to come would "seek and save" the lost. By using this phrase, knowing that His listeners knew the Scripture, Jesus communicated several things. To the people, He communicated, "I am the Messiah and also God." To the religious leaders, whose influence kept Zacchaeus out of the crowd, He said, "You have scattered and harmed God's flock." To Zacchaeus, He said, "You are one of God's lost sheep, and He still loves you."

Jesus best fit the type of rabbi believed to have *s'mikhah*, the authority to make new interpretations of the Torah. Whereas most teachers of the law could only teach accepted interpretations, teachers with authority could make new interpretations and pass legal judgments. Crowds were amazed because Jesus taught with authority (Matthew 7:28–29), and some people questioned His authority (Matthew 21:23–27).

Topic B: Confronting the "Gates of Hades"

Jesus took His disciples from their familiar, Jewish religious surroundings in Galilee to the equally religious, but pagan, city of Caesarea Philippi thirty miles away. Caesarea Philippi was a world center of Pan worship, boasting a yearly Pan festival and an assortment of other pagan shrines. Here Jesus gave them an essential lesson that would prepare them for their future ministry in a pagan world.

1. Why was Peter's use of the word "living" so significant when he declared Jesus to be "the Christ, the Son of the living God"? (See Matthew 16:13–16.)

   Suggested Responses: Jesus and His disciples were near the place called "the gates of Hades (hell)," where pagans worshiped man-made, "dead" gods. Peter's profession clearly identified Jesus as "the Son of the living God" in contrast to the "dead" gods of the Canaanites, Greeks, and Romans. Jesus was—and is—alive.

2. Read Matthew 16:17–19.

   a. Given the setting in which this conversation took place, what did Jesus mean by "on this rock I will build my church"?

      Suggested Responses: The prominent rock cliff at Caesarea Philippi represented everything evil in the world. It had many niches to hold idols and statues of pagan gods, and could have been viewed as the "rock of the gods." The message Jesus brought would replace the pagan worship represented by the cliff face. Jesus would build His church atop the ruins of the pagan world.

   Note: This is the first time Jesus referred to His "church," the new community He came to establish. Also, the "rock" on which the church is built has been the subject of much discussion throughout the history of Christianity. "This rock" has several meanings, one of which is the rock of the gods in Caesarea Philippi.

Artist's Rendering of Caesarea Philippi

Topic B: Confronting the "Gates of Hades"

Jesus took His disciples from their familiar, Jewish religious surroundings in Galilee to the equally religious, but pagan, city of Caesarea Philippi thirty miles away. Caesarea Philippi was a world center of Pan worship, boasting a yearly Pan festival and an assortment of other pagan shrines. Here Jesus gave them an essential lesson that would prepare them for their future ministry in a pagan world.

1. Why was Peter's use of the word "living" so significant when he declared Jesus to be "the Christ, the Son of the living God"? (See Matthew 16:13–16.)

Artist's Rendering of Caesarea Philippi

22

Faith Lessons on the Early Church

2. Read Matthew 16:17–19.

a. Given the setting in which this conversation took place, what did Jesus mean by "on this rock I will build my church"?

b. Since the cave at the base of the cliff was called the "gates of Hades," what did Jesus mean when He said, "I will build my church, and the gates of Hades will not overcome it"?

3. Read Mark 8:34–9:1.

a. What types of people were probably present when Jesus addressed the crowd near Caesarea Philippi?

DID YOU KNOW?
"The gates of Hades," a phrase found in Matthew 16:18, can be translated as "hell." Hades, called *Sheol* in the Old Testament Hebrew, is the place where departed spirits live. Apparently it was frequently used as a synonym for hell. (See Psalm 9:17; 55:15; 116:3.)

b. Since the cave at the base of the cliff was called the "gates of Hades," what did Jesus mean when He said, "I will build my church, and the gates of Hades will not overcome it"?

Suggested Responses: The mission of the church is to challenge and overcome the pagan values of our world. Thus the church is to be on the offensive, attacking the strongholds of evil and gaining victory over them, rather than on the defensive. Even the gates of Hades itself cannot stand against Jesus and His followers.

✏ **3.**   Read Mark 8:34–9:1.

a. What types of people were probably present when Jesus addressed the crowd near Caesarea Philippi?

Suggested Response: In addition to Jesus' disciples, most of the people who came to Caesarea Philippi were pagans who came to worship the fertility gods.

b. When Jesus invited the crowd to "come after" Him—to be His disciples, to be like Him—what did He tell them was required?

Suggested Responses: He required an all-out commitment. They needed to "deny" themselves, to stop giving in to their passions, and follow Him. They needed to know Him so that they could be like Him.

c. What would the term "deny" have meant to people who worshiped Pan and other false gods? (See also 1 Peter 4:3–4 and 1 John 2:15–17.)

Suggested Responses: If they chose to follow Jesus, they could no longer attempt to find meaning, purpose, and salvation by satisfying their most base, human lusts. Instead, they needed to find meaning and purpose in their relationship with God through Jesus Christ.

d. How did Jesus' strong words about being ashamed relate to how the disciples may have felt when Jesus confronted the pagan crowd? (See Mark 8:38.)

Suggested Responses: The disciples may well have wished that Jesus hadn't drawn so much attention to Himself—or to them. So Jesus strongly emphasized how important it was for them to stand unashamed as they presented His message to the world. This lesson helped prepare them to preach boldly to the pagan cultures of Asia Minor.

DID YOU KNOW?

"The gates of Hades," a phrase found in Matthew 16:18, can be translated as "hell." Hades, called *Sheol* in the Old Testament Hebrew, is the place where departed spirits live. Apparently it was frequently used as a synonym for hell. (See Psalm 9:17; 55:15; 116:3.)

2. Read Matthew 16:17–19.

   a. Given the setting in which this conversation took place, what did Jesus mean by "on this rock I will build my church"?

   b. Since the cave at the base of the cliff was called the "gates of Hades," what did Jesus mean when He said, "I will build my church, and the gates of Hades will not overcome it"?

3. Read Mark 8:34–9:1.

   a. What types of people were probably present when Jesus addressed the crowd near Caesarea Philippi?

DID YOU KNOW?
"The gates of Hades," a phrase found in Matthew 16:18, can be translated as "hell." Hades, called *Sheol* in the Old Testament Hebrew, is the place where departed spirits live. Apparently it was frequently used as a synonym for hell. (See Psalm 9:17; 55:15; 116:3.)

   b. When Jesus invited the crowd to "come after" Him—to be His disciples, to be like Him—what did He tell them was required?

   c. What would the term "deny" have meant to people who worshiped Pan and other false gods? (See also 1 Peter 4:3–4 and 1 John 2:15–17.)

   d. How did Jesus' strong words about being ashamed relate to how the disciples may have felt when Jesus confronted the pagan crowd? (See Mark 8:38.)

PLANNING NOTES:

DATA FILE

Pagan Worship by the Cave in Caesarea Philippi

The Grotto of Pan

At the foot of one of the ridges of Mount Hermon in northern Israel stands a 100-foot cliff that for centuries held great significance to pagan worshipers. Here, an underground river (one of the fountainheads of the Jordan River) flowed from a large, deep cave named the Grotto of Pan. The cave was also known as the "gates of Hades" (hell) because pagan people believed that their gods used this cave to travel to and from the underworld.

As part of their fertility rituals, worshipers carved small niches on the cliff face to hold statues or idols of their gods. These included Pan and his sexual partners (nymphs) as well as other goddesses of fertility cults such as Nemesis from Phoenicia—the home of Asherah and Baal. Idols of Athena and Aphrodite have been unearthed at this site, and Baal may have been worshiped here as well.

Several hundred years before Jesus visited this area with His disciples, Greek soldiers of Alexander the Great built a shrine dedicated to Pan—the fertility god of mountains and forests—on the flat area in front of the cliff face. A thirty-by-forty-five-foot platform served as the sacred place for Pan. Nearby, a Pan statue stood in a vaulted, artificial cave that contained niches holding the statues of nymphs who supposedly had sexual relations with Pan.

In front of the cave, about 20 B.C., Herod the Great built a small, thirty-by-sixty-foot temple of white marble dedicated to Emperor Augustus. During religious rites, animals were sacrificed and thrown into the cave. If the water rushing out contained blood, the gods had rejected the sacrifice. This temple, which honored a human who called himself a god, greatly offended Jewish people who followed the Torah (such as the disciples).

Near the cliff in which the cave was located, Herod the Great's son, Herod Phillip, built his capital city during Jesus' lifetime. He also enlarged the religious shrines. After Jesus' time, this location continued to be a focal point of pagan worship. A fifteen-by-forty-eight-foot Nemesis shrine, for example, was built to honor one of the nymphs of Pan—the goddess of revenge.

Pagan God Niche

Emperor Trajan (A.D. 98–117) built a thirty-five-by-fifty-foot temple dedicated to Zeus in this same area. And, about A.D. 220, the forty-eight-by-sixty-foot Goat Shrine and the thirty-five-by-twenty-two-foot Court of the Dancing Goats were built. In both of these, worshipers feasted on sacrificed (possibly raw) meat, made sacrifices to Pan and other pagan deities,

observed mating goats, and held religious celebrations. Sexual rituals (maybe even sexual relations between humans and goats) probably took place here as well. Nothing could have been more offensive to people who believed in God.

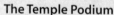

The Temple Podium

DATA FILE

Pagan Worship by the Cave in Caesarea Philippi

At the foot of one of the ridges of Mount Hermon in northern Israel stands a 100-foot cliff that for centuries held great significance to pagan worshipers. Here, an underground river (one of the fountainheads of the Jordan River) flowed from a large, deep cave named the Grotto of Pan. The cave

The Grotto of Pan

was also known as the "gates of Hades" (hell) because pagan people believed that their gods used this cave to travel to and from the underworld.

As part of their fertility rituals, worshipers carved small niches on the cliff face to hold statues or idols of their gods. These included Pan and his sexual partners (nymphs) as well as other goddesses of fertility cults such as Nemesis from Phoenicia—the home of Asherah and Baal. Idols of Athena and Aphrodite have been unearthed at this site, and Baal may have been worshiped here as well.

Several hundred years before Jesus visited this area with His disciples, Greek soldiers of Alexander the Great built a shrine dedicated to Pan—the fertility god of mountains and forests—on the flat area in front of the cliff face. A thirty-by-forty-five-foot platform served as the sacred place for Pan. Nearby, a Pan statue stood in a vaulted, artificial cave that contained niches holding the statues of nymphs who supposedly had sexual relations with Pan.

In front of the cave, about 20 B.C., Herod the Great built a small, thirty-by-sixty-foot temple of white marble dedicated to emperor Augustus. During religious rites, animals were sacrificed and thrown into the cave. If the water rushing out contained blood, the gods had rejected the sacrifice.

This temple, which honored a human who called himself a god, greatly offended Jewish people who followed the Torah (such as the disciples).

Pagan God Niche

Near the cliff in which the cave was located, Herod the Great's son, Herod Phillip, built his capital city during Jesus' lifetime. He also enlarged the religious shrines. After Jesus' time, this location continued to be a focal point of pagan worship. A fifteen-by-forty-eight-foot Nemesis shrine, for example, was built to honor one of the nymphs of Pan—the goddess of revenge.

Emperor Trajan (A.D. 98–117) built a thirty-five-by-fifty-foot temple dedicated to Zeus in this same area. And, about A.D. 220, the forty-eight-by-sixty-foot Goat Shrine and the thirty-five-by-twenty-two-foot Court of the Dancing Goats were built. In both of these, worshipers feasted on sacrificed (possibly raw) meat, made sacrifices to Pan and other pagan deities, observed mating goats, and held religious celebrations. Sexual rituals (maybe even sexual relations between humans and goats) probably took place here as well. Nothing could have been more offensive to people who believed in God.

The Temple Podium

> ### WORTH OBSERVING . . .
>
> #### The Meaning of the "Rock"
> Throughout church history, there has been discussion and debate on exactly what Jesus meant when He said, "on this rock I will build my church" (Matthew 16:18). As we've explored in this session, the cliff face in Caesarea Philippi that was used for centuries in idol worship provides yet another metaphor for the "rock" Jesus mentioned. In this setting, the "rock" can mean the "rock" of pagan values and dead idolatry that was so prominent in Caesarea Philippi. Jesus, then, was saying that His church would replace those values. Two other viewpoints within the traditional understanding of the meaning of the "rock" are:
>
> 1. The "rock" is the confession of Peter that Jesus is Christ (i.e., Christ, the Son of the living God, is the foundation of the church. See Acts 4:10–11 and 1 Corinthians 3:10–15).
> 2. The "rock" is Peter, whose confession on behalf of the other disciples acknowledged the truth that Jesus is Messiah.

Topic C: Jesus' Ascension

The ascension of Jesus to heaven, as the disciples watched on the Mount of Olives (Acts 1:9–12), was a key lesson in their preparation for future ministry. To the Jews, the ascension clearly declared God's ultimate victory over the world, including the defeat of Rome and paganism. But the ascension also conveyed a radical message to the Gentile world, one that would directly challenge emperor worship in Asia Minor.

1. Read Daniel's vision, found in Daniel 7:13–14. How did Jesus' ascension relate to this prophecy?

    Suggested Responses: As Daniel had prophesied, Jesus—the Messiah, the Son of Man—returned to heaven to be with God and was given authority, glory, and sovereign power. Thus, Jesus' ascension fulfilled Daniel's prophecy.

2. As religious Jewish men, the disciples would have known about Daniel's vision of the Messiah and the coming of God's kingdom. Note the similarities between Daniel's vision (Daniel 7:13–14) and Jesus' last teachings and His ascension as recorded in the following passages. Also note the impact these events had on the disciples.

Passage	Similarities	Impact on Disciples
Matthew 28:16–20	*Jesus said He had been given all authority in heaven and on earth.*	*Because of Jesus' authority, they were to go and make disciples.*
Luke 24:50–53	*Jesus was taken up to heaven before their eyes.*	*They went to the temple to worship and praise God.*
Acts 1:6–11	*Jesus was taken up into the clouds, Jesus talked to them about His kingdom.*	*They were reassured that Jesus' kingdom was established, that He would come back for them, that they were to be His witnesses.*

WORTH OBSERVING . . .

The Meaning of the "Rock"

Throughout church history, there has been discussion and debate on exactly what Jesus meant when He said, "on this rock I will build my church" (Matthew 16:18). As we've explored in this session, the cliff face in Caesarea Philippi that was used for centuries in idol worship provides yet another metaphor for the "rock" Jesus mentioned. In this setting, the "rock" can mean the "rock" of pagan values and dead idolatry that was so prominent in Caesarea Philippi. Jesus, then, was saying that His church would replace those values. Two other viewpoints within the traditional understanding of the meaning of the "rock" are:

1. The "rock" is the confession of Peter that Jesus is Christ (i.e., Christ, the Son of the living God, is the foundation of the church. See Acts 4:10–11 and 1 Corinthians 3:10–15).

2. The "rock" is Peter, whose confession on behalf of the other disciples acknowledged the truth that Jesus is Messiah.

Topic C: Jesus' Ascension

The ascension of Jesus to heaven, as the disciples watched on the Mount of Olives (Acts 1:9–12), was a key lesson in their preparation for future ministry. To the Jews, the ascension clearly declared God's ultimate victory over the world, including the defeat of Rome and paganism. But the ascension also conveyed a radical message to the Gentile world, one that would directly challenge emperor worship in Asia Minor.

1. Read Daniel's vision, found in Daniel 7:13–14. How did Jesus' ascension relate to this prophecy?

2. As religious Jewish men, the disciples would have known about Daniel's vision of the Messiah and the coming of God's kingdom. Note the similarities between Daniel's vision (Daniel 7:13–14) and Jesus' last teachings and His ascension as recorded in the following passages. Also note the impact these events had on the disciples.

Passage	Similarities	Impact on Disciples
Matthew 28:16–20		
Luke 24:50–53		
Acts 1:6–11		

3. What did Jesus tell His disciples just before He ascended? (See Matthew 28:16–20 and Acts 1:3–9.)

4. What did the disciples witness firsthand, and how would news of this event be received by the Roman world?

The Districts of Jerusalem

3. What did Jesus tell His disciples just before He ascended? (See Matthew 28:16–20 and Acts 1:3–9).

Suggested Responses: Jesus told them that they would be witnesses for Him throughout the world; that they were to be His disciples, baptizing and teaching people to obey His commandments; that they were to wait in Jerusalem for the power of the Holy Spirit that God would give to them; that He had been given all authority in heaven and on earth; that He would be with them; etc.

4. What did the disciples witness firsthand, and how would news of this event be received by the Roman world?

Suggested Responses: The disciples saw Jesus ascend to heaven and also heard two angels affirm what had happened. What they had seen was in opposition to what the Roman emperors wanted people to believe—that Caesar is God. After all, if Jesus is Lord, then Caesar is not God and is a fraud. This was a powerful challenge to the Roman world.

Note: When Jesus ascended, the deification of Roman emperors was just beginning. So His ascension planted a radical message that would explode on the world scene. In Asia Minor, where emperor worship occurred the earliest and became the strongest, the message of Jesus' ascension led to the execution of most of the disciples.

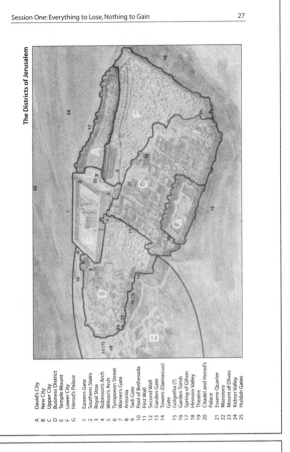

The Districts of Jerusalem

A   David's City
B   New City
C   Upper City
D   Business District
E   Temple Mount
F   Lower City
G   Herod's Palace

1   Eastern Gate
2   Southern Stairs
3   Royal Stoa
4   Robinson's Arch
5   Wilson's Arch
6   Tyropoeon Street
7   Warren's Gate
8   Antonia
9   Tadi Gate
10   Pool of Bethesada
11   First Wall
12   Second Wall
13   Garden Gate
14   Towers (Damascus) Gate
15   Golgotha (?)
16   Garden Tomb
17   Spring of Gihon
18   Hinnom Valley
19   Theatre
20   Citadel and Herod's Palace
21   Essene Quarter
22   Mansions
23   Mount of Olives
24   Kidron Valley
25   Huldah Gates

28   Faith Lessons on the Early Church

2. As religious Jewish men, the disciples would have known about Daniel's vision of the Messiah and the coming of God's kingdom. Note the similarities between Daniel's vision (Daniel 7:13–14) and Jesus' last teachings and His ascension as recorded in the following passages. Also note the impact these events had on the disciples.

Passage	Similarities	Impact on Disciples
Matthew 28:16–20		
Luke 24:50–53		
Acts 1:6–11		

3. What did Jesus tell His disciples just before He ascended? (See Matthew 28:16–20 and Acts 1:3–9.)

4. What did the disciples witness firsthand, and how would news of this event be received by the Roman world?

Topic D: The Power of *Talmidim*

Jesus calls His followers to be *talmidim* who make *talmidim*. This means His disciples are to seek to be like Him. They are to develop relationships with other people who imitate them as they imitate Jesus. One reason the gospel spread so rapidly during the time of the early church was because Jesus' disciples had a passion to be like Jesus and put into practice what they had been taught by Jesus or by other Christians. Notice how Jesus prepared His *talmidim* and how they responded.

1. Instruction and practice are an important part of any training effort. During His ministry on earth, Jesus sent disciples out into the world to minister to others on at least two occasions. In each instance note His instructions, what the disciples did, and the result.

   a. The Twelve (see Luke 9:1–6).

   Suggested Responses: Jesus gave them power and authority to drive out demons, heal the sick, and preach the kingdom of God. He told them to take no physical provisions for the journey, but to rely on the hospitality of those who welcomed them. He told them to leave those who did not welcome them. They did it.

   b. The seventy-two (see Luke 10:1–12, 17–20).

   Suggested Responses: Jesus sent them out ahead of Him, two by two. He told them to take no physical provisions for the journey but to rely on the hospitality of those who welcomed them. They were to heal the sick and preach the kingdom of God but were to leave those who did not welcome them. They did it and were filled with joy. Upon their return, Jesus rejoices with them and reminded them of the authority He had given to them and of their true reason to rejoice.

2. In Matthew 28:16–20, Jesus gave His disciples their instructions. Note the way in which they carried them out.

   a. Acts 26:19–29

   Suggested Responses: Paul's defense of himself before King Agrippa and Festus is to preach the gospel and to appeal to his listeners to become like him.

   b. 1 Corinthians 4:15–17

   Suggested Responses: Paul reminds his readers that he is their "father" in the gospel and on that basis appeals to them to imitate him. He also sends Timothy to be a visible reminder of living out life in Christ.

   c. 1 Thessalonians 1:6–7

   Suggested Responses: Paul reminds his readers that they welcomed the message of Christ and became imitators of the Lord and models for other believers.

   d. Hebrews 6:12; 13:7

   Suggested Responses: The writer of Hebrews reminds his readers to imitate the life of Christ as demonstrated by those who brought the message to them.

Topic D: The Power of *Talmidim*

Jesus calls His followers to be *talmidim* who make *talmidim*. This means His disciples are to seek to be like Him. They are to develop relationships with other people who imitate them as they imitate Jesus. One reason the gospel spread so rapidly during the time of the early church was because Jesus' disciples had a passion to be like Jesus and put into practice what they had been taught by Jesus or by other Christians. Notice how Jesus prepared His *talmidim* and how they responded.

1. Instruction and practice are an important part of any training effort. During His ministry on earth, Jesus sent disciples out into the world to minister to others on at least two occasions. In each instance note His instructions, what the disciples did, and the result.

    a. The Twelve (see Luke 9:1–6).

    b. The seventy-two (see Luke 10:1–12, 17–20).

2. In Matthew 28:16–20, Jesus gave His disciples their instructions. Note the way in which they carried them out.

    a. Acts 26:19–29

    b. 1 Corinthians 4:15–17

    c. 1 Thessalonians 1:6–7

    d. Hebrews 6:12; 13:7

WORTH OBSERVING . . .

The Relationship That Can Change the World

Jesus' disciples, the ones He called into relationship with Him as *talmidim*, made such an impact on the province of Asia Minor—the most pagan of all the Roman provinces—that it became the most Christian province in the Roman Empire. Jesus desires the same kind of relationship with His disciples today. To have that kind of relationship in our world means that we must:

· Know God's Word and Jesus' interpretation of it.
· Be passionate in our devotion to that Word and Jesus' example.
· Follow Him even if we are not sure of the final destination.
· Live by His teaching, which means we must know that teaching well.
· Be obsessed with being like Him as much as is humanly possible.
· Develop meaningful relationships with others so that they will observe us and seek to imitate our love, devotion to God, and our Jesus-like lifestyle. (See 1 Corinthians 2:16; 11:1; Galatians 3:26–27.)

By God's grace, people with totally committed relationships to Christ can change the most pagan culture—including our own.

WORTH OBSERVING . . .

The Relationship That Can Change the World

Jesus' disciples, the ones He called into relationship with Him as *talmidim,* made such an impact on the province of Asia Minor—the most pagan of all the Roman provinces—that it became the most Christian province in the Roman Empire. Jesus desires the same kind of relationship with His disciples today. To have that kind of relationship in our world means that we must:

- Know God's Word and Jesus' interpretation of it.
- Be passionate in our devotion to that Word and Jesus' example.
- Follow Him even if we are not sure of the final destination.
- Live by His teaching, which means we must know that teaching well.
- Be obsessed with being like Him as much as is humanly possible.
- Develop meaningful relationships with others so that they will observe us and seek to imitate our love, devotion to God, and our Jesus-like lifestyle. (See 1 Corinthians 2:16; 11:1; Galatians 3:26–27.)

By God's grace, people with totally committed relationships to Christ can change the most pagan culture—including our own.

DATA FILE

The Amazing Galileans

Jesus focused His ministry in one small place in Israel: Galilee, in the three cities of Korazin, Capernaum, and Bethsaida. Although many people today assume that Galileans were simple, uneducated peasants who lived in an isolated area, the truth is they interacted more with the world than the Jews of Jerusalem. After all, the Via Maris trade route passed through Galilee, exposing them to many different peoples and cultures.

The Galileans were also the most religious Jews in the world during Jesus' time. They revered and knew the Scriptures well. They were passionately committed to living out their faith and passing their faith, knowledge, and lifestyle on to their children. This led to the establishment of vibrant religious communities; a strong commitment to families and country; and active participation in the local synagogues—the community centers of that day. In fact, more famous Jewish teachers came from Galilee than from anywhere else.

The Galileans resisted the pagan influences of Hellenism far longer than their Judean counterparts, and when the great revolt against the Romans and their collaborators finally occurred (A.D. 66–74), it began among the Galileans.

Clearly God carefully prepared the environment in which Jesus was born and reared so that He would have exactly the context He needed in order to present His message of *malchut Shemayim*—the kingdom of heaven—effectively, and so that people would understand and join His new movement.

A deeper knowledge of Galilee and its people helps us understand the great faith and courage of His disciples, who left Galilee and shared the good news with the world. (Evidence indicates that Judas Iscariot was apparently the only non-Galilean among Jesus' twelve, closest disciples.) The disciples' courage, the message they taught, the methods they used, and their complete devotion to God and His Word were born in Galilee's religious communities.

b. 1 Corinthians 4:15–17

c. 1 Thessalonians 1:6–7

d. Hebrews 6:12; 13:7

WORTH OBSERVING . . .

The Relationship That Can Change the World

Jesus' disciples, the ones He called into relationship with Him as *talmidim*, made such an impact on the province of Asia Minor—the most pagan of all the Roman provinces—that it became the most Christian province in the Roman Empire. Jesus desires the same kind of relationship with His disciples today. To have that kind of relationship in our world means that we must:

- Know God's Word and Jesus' interpretation of it.
- Be passionate in our devotion to that Word and Jesus' example.
- Follow Him even if we are not sure of the final destination.
- Live by His teaching, which means we must know that teaching well.
- Be obsessed with being like Him as much as is humanly possible.
- Develop meaningful relationships with others so that they will observe us and seek to imitate our love, devotion to God, and our Jesus-like lifestyle. (See 1 Corinthians 2:16; 11:1; Galatians 3:26–27.)

By God's grace, people with totally committed relationships to Christ can change the most pagan culture—including our own.

DATA FILE

The Amazing Galileans

Jesus focused His ministry in one small place in Israel: Galilee, in the three cities of Korazin, Capernaum, and Bethsaida. Although many people today assume that Galileans were simple, uneducated peasants who lived in an isolated area, the truth is they interacted more with the world than the Jews of Jerusalem. After all, the Via Maris trade route passed through Galilee, exposing them to many different peoples and cultures.

The Galileans were also the most religious Jews in the world during Jesus' time. They revered and knew the Scriptures well. They were passionately committed to living out their faith and passing their faith, knowledge, and lifestyle on to their children. This led to the establishment of vibrant religious communities; a strong commitment to families and country; and active participation in the local synagogues—the community centers of that day. In fact, more famous Jewish teachers came from Galilee than from anywhere else.

The Galileans resisted the pagan influences of Hellenism far longer than their Judean counterparts, and when the great revolt against the Romans and their collaborators finally occurred (A.D. 66–74), it began among the Galileans.

Clearly God carefully prepared the environment in which Jesus was born and reared so that He would have exactly the context He needed in order to present His message of *malchut Shemayim*—the kingdom of heaven—effectively, and so that people would understand and join His new movement.

A deeper knowledge of Galilee and its people helps us understand the great faith and courage of His disciples, who left Galilee and shared the good news with the world. (Evidence indicates that Judas Iscariot was apparently the only non-Galilean among Jesus' twelve, closest disciples.) The disciples' courage, the message they taught, the methods they used, and their complete devotion to God and His Word were born in Galilee's religious communities.

PLANNING NOTES:

Topic E: Idolatry in Northern Israel

Although God gave the tribe of Dan a designated territory in the Shephelah between the coastal plain and the mountains of Judea, they did not capture this land in the name of the Lord. Instead, they packed up their families and settled near the northern border of Israel in an area that was widely known as a pagan worship center.

1. What did the Danites do when they discovered that a house in this region had a Levite priest as well as an idol, carved image, and other articles of pagan worship? (See Judges 18:1–2, 11–20.)

   Suggested Response: The Danites took the articles of pagan worship and invited the priest to go with them, which he did.

2. How did the Danites go about establishing their homeland? (See Judges 18:27–31.)

   Suggested Responses: The Danites attacked the peaceful and unsuspecting people of Laish and burned down their city. Then they rebuilt the city, named it Dan, and, with the assistance of their own priests, began worshiping idols.

3. After Solomon's death, the nation of Israel split into two kingdoms—Israel in the north and Judah in the south. What did Jeroboam, king of Israel, do to preserve his kingdom? (See 1 Kings 12:26–32.)

   Suggested Responses: Jeroboam was concerned that if the people worshiped God in Jerusalem, he would lose his kingdom. So he made two golden calves for the people to worship, saying that the calves had brought them out of Egypt. He also built shrines on high places, appointed priests who were not Levites, and established festivals at which the people sacrificed to idols, etc.

4. What happened in Israel as a result of what King Jeroboam did in Dan? (See 1 Kings 16:15–19, 23–26, 29–33.)

   Suggested Responses: Future kings of Israel continued to commit the same sins of idolatry that Jeroboam initiated. Their idolatry greatly angered God.

5. When God sent pagan nations to punish His people for their idol worship, what happened to the city of Dan? (See 1 Kings 15:18–20.)

   Suggested Response: Ben-Hadad conquered the city of Dan.

> Signal the groups when one minute remains so that they may wrap up their discovery time.

Topic E: Idolatry in Northern Israel

Although God gave the tribe of Dan a designated territory in the Shephelah between the coastal plain and the mountains of Judea, they did not capture this land in the name of the Lord. Instead, they packed up their families and settled near the northern border of Israel in an area that was widely known as a pagan worship center.

1. What did the Danites do when they discovered that a house in this region had a Levite priest as well as an idol, carved image, and other articles of pagan worship? (See Judges 18:1–2, 11–20.)

2. How did the Danites go about establishing their homeland? (See Judges 18:27–31.)

3. After Solomon's death, the nation of Israel split into two kingdoms—Israel in the north and Judah in the south. What did Jeroboam, king of Israel, do to preserve his kingdom? (See 1 Kings 12:26–32.)

4. What happened in Israel as a result of what King Jeroboam did in Dan? (See 1 Kings 16:15–19, 23–26, 29–33.)

5. When God sent pagan nations to punish His people for their idol worship, what happened to the city of Dan? (See 1 Kings 15:18–20.)

faith Lesson

Time for Reflection

Read the following passage of Scripture and take the next few minutes to consider the ways in which Jesus prepared His disciples to fulfill the mission He had for them.

> Then the eleven disciples went to Galilee, to the mountain where Jesus had told them to go. When they saw him, they worshiped him; but some doubted. Then Jesus came to them and said, "All authority in heaven and on earth has been given to me. Therefore go and make disciples of all nations, baptizing them in the name of the Father and of the Son and of the Holy Spirit, and teaching them to obey everything I have commanded you. And surely I am with you always, to the very end of the age."
>
> MATTHEW 28:16–20

PLANNING NOTES:

faith Lesson

Time for Reflection (2 minutes)

It's time for each of us to think quietly about how Jesus prepared His disciples to fulfill the mission He had for them. On page 33 of the Participant's Guide, you'll find a passage of Scripture. Let's each read this passage silently and take the next few minutes to consider the question that follows.

Please do not talk during this time. It's a time when we can reflect on today's lesson and how it applies to our lives.

> The Scripture passage and questions are reproduced in their entirety in the Participant's Guide on pages 33–34.

> Then the eleven disciples went to Galilee, to the mountain where Jesus had told them to go. When they saw him, they worshiped him; but some doubted. Then Jesus came to them and said, "All authority in heaven and on earth has been given to me. Therefore go and make disciples of all nations, baptizing them in the name of the Father and of the Son and of the Holy Spirit, and teaching them to obey everything I have commanded you. And surely I am with you always, to the very end of the age." (Matthew 28:16–20)

These words, spoken by Jesus shortly before His ascension, conveyed a powerful and compelling message to His disciples. Jesus sent them out with "all authority." He clearly told them to teach obedience and "make disciples of all nations." And He promised to be with them always. Take some time to prayerfully consider not only what these words meant to the disciples who had lived as *talmidim* of Jesus the rabbi, but what they mean to you as you go out into your world.

Action Points (2 minutes)

> *The following points are reproduced on page 34 of the Participant's Guide.*

Now it's time to wrap up our session.

> Give participants a moment to transition from their thoughtfulness to giving you their full attention.

I'd like to take a moment to summarize the key points we explored. After I have reviewed these points, I will give you a moment to jot down an action step (or steps) that you will commit to this week as a result of what you have learned today.

> Read the following points and pause afterward so that participants can consider and write out their commitment.

4. What happened in Israel as a result of what King Jeroboam did in Dan? (See 1 Kings 16:15–19, 23–26, 29–33.)

5. When God sent pagan nations to punish His people for their idol worship, what happened to the city of Dan? (See 1 Kings 15:18–20.)

faith Lesson

Time for Reflection

Read the following passage of Scripture and take the next few minutes to consider the ways in which Jesus prepared His disciples to fulfill the mission He had for them.

> Then the eleven disciples went to Galilee, to the mountain where Jesus had told them to go. When they saw him, they worshiped him; but some doubted. Then Jesus came to them and said, "All authority in heaven and on earth has been given to me. Therefore go and make disciples of all nations, baptizing them in the name of the Father and of the Son and of the Holy Spirit, and teaching them to obey everything I have commanded you. And surely I am with you always, to the very end of the age."
>
> MATTHEW 28:16–20

These words, spoken by Jesus shortly before His ascension, conveyed a powerful and compelling message to His disciples. Jesus sent them out with "all authority." He clearly told them to teach obedience and "make disciples of all nations." And He promised to be with them always. Take some time to prayerfully consider not only what these words meant to the disciples who had lived as *talmidim* of Jesus the rabbi, but what they mean to you as you go out into your world.

Action Points

Take a moment to jot down an action step (or steps) that you will commit to this week as a result of what you have learned.

1. *As a rabbi, Jesus prepared His chosen disciples—His talmidim—to carry on His message after He was gone.* He lived in community with them, interpreting and modeling the Torah so that they would know how to live God's way. He taught them about His faith, which is a passionate commitment to act in accordance with what they believed.

   In what ways are you, or are you not, a true disciple of Jesus?

   As a disciple—a *talmid*—of Jesus, what are you willing to do this week in order to model Christ's love to an unbeliever?

1. *As a rabbi, Jesus prepared His chosen disciples—His* talmidim—*to carry on His message after He was gone.* He lived in community with them, interpreting and modeling the Torah so that they would know how to live God's way. He taught them about His faith, which is a passionate commitment to act in accordance with what they believed.

    In what ways are you, or are you not, a true disciple of Jesus?

    As a disciple—a *talmid*—of Jesus, what are you willing to do this week in order to model Christ's love to an unbeliever?

2. *Shortly before going to Jerusalem for the last time, Jesus took His disciples to Caesarea Philippi, a pagan worship center. Here, His disciples realized anew that He was the Messiah, the Son of the* living *God.* He also assured them that His church would triumph—even over the gates of Hades (hell). How important this truth would become when the disciples faced personal suffering, even martyrdom, because of their commitment to Him.

    Identify the "dead" gods and pagan values of our culture that need to be challenged and replaced with God's values.

    Today, through the power of the living God, we can share our faith even in the most difficult situations. We can overcome the "gates of hell" in our culture. In what specific way(s) can you effectively influence your culture by seeking to be like Jesus?

3. *As eyewitnesses of His ascension, the disciples were empowered to boldly proclaim the message of Jesus to their world.* For His last teaching, Jesus took His disciples to the Mount of Olives and reminded them that they were His witnesses to the world. Then, before their eyes, He ascended into heaven. This dramatic scene inspired them to go out and tell everyone about the living Messiah who will one day return to claim His own.

    Jesus' ascension greatly increased the faith of His disciples before they went out to fulfill their ministry in many nations. What difference does His ascension make to your faith?

    Is Jesus' ascension so real to you that you are willing to take the "heat" and proclaim the *living* Christ no matter what? In what ways does it empower you to face the "Asia Minors" in your culture with confidence and power?

These words, spoken by Jesus shortly before His ascension, conveyed a powerful and compelling message to His disciples. Jesus sent them out with "all authority." He clearly told them to teach obedience and "make disciples of all nations." And He promised to be with them always. Take some time to prayerfully consider not only what these words meant to the disciples who had lived as *talmidim* of Jesus the rabbi, but what they mean to you as you go out into your world.

Action Points

Take a moment to jot down an action step (or steps) that you will commit to this week as a result of what you have learned.

1. *As a rabbi, Jesus prepared His chosen disciples—His talmidim—to carry on His message after He was gone.* He lived in community with them, interpreting and modeling the Torah so that they would know how to live God's way. He taught them about His faith, which is a passionate commitment to act in accordance with what they believed.

   In what ways are you, or are you not, a true disciple of Jesus?

   As a disciple—a *talmid*—of Jesus, what are you willing to do this week in order to model Christ's love to an unbeliever?

2. *Shortly before going to Jerusalem for the last time, Jesus took His disciples to Caesarea Philippi, a pagan worship center. Here, His disciples realized anew that He was the Messiah, the Son of the living God.* He also assured them that His church would triumph—even over the gates of Hades (hell). How important this truth would become when the disciples faced personal suffering, even martyrdom, because of their commitment to Him.

   Identify the "dead" gods and pagan values of our culture that need to be challenged and replaced with God's values.

   Today, through the power of the living God, we can share our faith even in the most difficult situations. We can overcome the "gates of hell" in our culture. In what specific way(s) can you effectively influence your culture by seeking to be like Jesus?

3. *As eyewitnesses of His ascension, the disciples were empowered to boldly proclaim the message of Jesus to their world.* For His last teaching, Jesus took His disciples to the Mount of Olives and reminded them that they were His witnesses to the world. Then, before their eyes, He ascended into heaven. This dramatic scene inspired them to go out and tell everyone about the living Messiah who will one day return to claim His own.

Jesus' ascension greatly increased the faith of His disciples before they went out to fulfill their ministry in many nations. **What difference does His ascension make to your faith?**

Is Jesus' ascension so real to you that you are willing to take the "heat" and proclaim the *living* Christ no matter what? In what ways does it empower you to face the "Asia Minors" in your culture with confidence and power?

PLANNING NOTES:

closing prayer

Jesus, our risen Savior, is in heaven and desires that we be effective disciples wherever we are. Let's close in prayer now, thanking Him for giving us the power to confront evil and committing ourselves to live as His disciples.

Dear Lord Jesus, You taught Your disciples so much as You lived and ministered among them. By the time You ascended to Your throne in heaven, they had discovered that as talmidim of the living God, they could confront all evil—even the gates of Hades. Armed by Your Spirit and empowered by Your example, they went out to the most pagan and evil part of their world to proclaim your message. Help us to do no less. Give us the desire to be like You, to demonstrate Your love and proclaim Your message to spiritually needy people all around us—in our families and neighborhoods as well as in places that are foreign and frightening to us. Help us to be willing to confront evil in Your name, so that people can receive the real meaning and purpose that only You—the living Christ—can provide. In Your name we pray. Amen.

PLANNING NOTES:

The salt of the earth

Before you lead

Synopsis

Located on Mount Tmolus in southern Turkey, the city of Sardis stood at the crossroads of Asia Minor, the most prosperous, powerful, fertile, and pagan province of the entire Roman Empire. First-century Sardis had a unique blend of residents: faithful Jews and Christians who worshiped God blended with influential pagans who worshiped the Roman emperor and gods such as Artemis and Cybele. Sardis is of particular interest because it apparently had a very visible Christian church and because the apostle John issued a strong warning to them.

The city was probably occupied first by the Hittites, then by the Lydians. Around 550 B.C., the most famous Lydian king, Croesus (who was also believed to be the richest man in the world) was besieged by Cyrus the Persian. Croesus, who had become apathetic and lazy, fortified himself in the acropolis of Sardis, and Cyrus could not conquer him. Then one afternoon, a Persian soldier named Lagoras watched a Lydian soldier sneak down the back wall of Sardis to retrieve a helmet. Deducing that a secret trail existed, Lagoras told Cyrus, whose army crawled up that little path at night and conquered the city. Croesus hadn't been as careful about the city's defense as he should have been, and he and his people paid for that mistake with their lives. Centuries later, the Greeks were able to capture the city through a similar lapse in vigilance on the part of the people defending Sardis.

Ray Vander Laan points out this story because it appears to relate closely to the strong metaphor the apostle John used when he warned the church of Sardis: "I know your deeds; you have a reputation of being alive, but you are dead. Wake up! . . . But if you do not wake up, I will come like a thief, and you will not know at what time I will come to you" (Revelation 3:1–3). Given the history of their city, the Christians in Sardis understood this imagery all too well. If John was drawing on that experience, he was probably implying that they needed to stay watchful and alert in order to maintain their Christian walk.

Although no one knows who planted the church in Sardis, it certainly was in a significant metropolitan area where it could influence the culture. The fact that a strong Jewish presence already existed there gave the early Christian missionaries a good place to start. The Jews expected a Messiah who would not only come to redeem but to bring morality, truth, and justice—concepts that were foreign to the pagan religions of the area.

Archaeological evidence suggests that both Jews and Christians openly displayed their faith in Sardis:

- Jewish or Christian symbols—crosses, menorahs, rings with crosses in them, and even the "fish" symbol—have been discovered in a number of the shops.
- A number of defaced pagan articles have been found. In one instance, a pagan goddess had been removed from the back of a lion-shaped lamp, which had then been patched and reused. In another place, large Christian crosses had been chiseled over pagan symbols on tombstones that had been reused to make a dye vat.

Thus it appears that God-fearing shop owners in that extremely pagan culture were making a clear statement that they stood for God and were attempting to reclaim anti-God, pagan articles.

One of the most impressive ruins in Sardis is that of the Greek gymnasium and Roman bathhouse. The gymnasium was the center of Greek culture, the means by which they passed on their Hellenistic worldview that the human being, not God, was the center of the universe. Within the gymnasium, students trained their bodies and minds. They read literature about the Greek gods and studied mathematics, philosophy, and medicine. They also enjoyed the pleasures and vices of the Roman baths.

Yet, in the corner of that immoral, self-glorifying gymnasium, archaeologists have uncovered the largest synagogue of that time period ever found! The presence of the synagogue within the gymnasium, as well as the presence of defaced pagan symbols within the synagogue—a public fountain, a table with Roman eagles, and pairs of lions that typically represented the goddess Cybele—beg the question "why?" Did the Jews of Sardis place their synagogue in the gymnasium in order to influence the culture, or had they so adopted the pagan way of life that they saw no discrepancy between worshiping God and participating in the activities of the gymnasium?

A similar question arises when Ray takes his viewers to the most ancient ruins in Sardis—a large, open-air shrine initially consecrated to Cybele. When the Greeks arrived in about 330 B.C., they built a huge temple to Artemis, their goddess of fertility, and absorbed the grossly immoral worship of Cybele into their worship. The ruins of this temple, which was one of the seven largest Greek temples in the world, stands as a testimony to the popularity and power of the Artemis cult.

Yet, in one corner of this temple stands a tiny Christian church that was built during the fourth century! Why did Christians build a church inside a pagan temple? Were they seeking to reclaim the temple, which was probably nearly abandoned at that time, for God? Or had they become so comfortable in their pagan world that their worship of God blended in with the pagan worship that surrounded them?

Ray concludes this video by pointing out that we don't know the answers to these questions, but they ought to cause us to consider our own faithfulness to Jesus' command to be the "salt of the earth" (Matthew 5:13). He goes on to explain how the people of the ancient Middle East mixed salt with animal droppings in order to make the droppings burn hotter and longer in their ovens. He suggests that in a similar way Christians are to mix in with the ugliness of the world's culture, to put our faith on the line in the midst of pagan culture and bring the message of Jesus to a sick society. We are to build God's kingdom at the heart of our cultures, our communities, and our world, but we must be careful not to compromise our faith in the process. We must remain distinctively salt.

Key Points of This Lesson

1. *Jesus sent His disciples out to be "salt" in an evil world.* They were to go into the world and live out the good news without compromise. They were to retain their distinctiveness without isolating themselves from unbelievers.

   The evidence of Sardis raises the question of whether the Jews and Christians of that city were a distinctive influence among their pagan neighbors or whether they compromised their calling and lost the distinctive beliefs and lifestyle that are essential to faith in God.

2. *John used a well-known, local, historical metaphor when he warned the Christians of Sardis to influence their world without compromising with it.* "I know your deeds," he wrote, "you have a reputation of being alive, but you are dead. Wake up! . . . but if you do not wake up, I will come like a thief, and you will not know at what time I will come to you" (Revelation 3:1–3).

   This reminder applies to Christians today as well. We must be careful to stay watchful, alert, and alive to what's going on in our Christian walk. Otherwise, we might become apathetic or make a mistake that would cause our witness to a watching world to collapse.

3. *Worldview is important.* The Greeks in Sardis taught Hellenism, which glorified human beings and considered them to be the center of the universe, the source of all wisdom. This view stands in opposition to the biblical worldview that recognizes God as Lord of the universe and the source of all truth.

   The great spiritual struggle throughout human history has been whether or not people choose to recognize God as the supreme being or insist on declaring themselves as the ultimate being.

Session Outline (53 minutes)

  I. **Introduction** (4 minutes)

  Welcome

  What's to Come

  Questions to Think About

  II. **Show Video "The Salt of the Earth"** (26 minutes)

  III. **Group Discovery** (15 minutes)

  Video Highlights

  Small Group Bible Discovery

  IV. **Faith Lesson** (7 minutes)

  Time for Reflection

  Action Points

  V. **Closing Prayer** (1 minute)

Materials

No additional materials are needed for this session. Simply view the video prior to leading the session so you are familiar with its main points.

The salt of the earth

introduction

Welcome

> Assemble the participants together. Welcome them to session two of *Faith Lessons on the Early Church.*

What's to Come

In this session, we'll consider what it meant for God's people to be the "salt of the earth" in the ancient city of Sardis, located in what is now Turkey. We'll go into the shops, the gymnasium, and a pagan temple to discover the ways in which religious Jews and early Christians demonstrated their faith in the midst of a very pagan culture. The evidence we see will cause us to wonder whether God's people in Sardis influenced their culture for Him, or simply compromised with the popular culture. This message is highly relevant because we, too, must determine how to demonstrate our faith in an increasingly pagan society.

Questions to Think About

> *Participant's Guide page 37.*
>
> Ask each question and solicit a few responses from group members.

1. Describe the areas or ways in which you find it easy to compromise your faith and fit in with secular culture. What makes it difficult to stand up for Christ in these situations?

   Suggested Responses: Encourage participants to express their fears and desires, their lack of diligence or concern, their lack of knowledge, their lack of love and devotion for God, etc.

2. Describe the type of involvement in the secular world and with secular people that you as a Christian must have in order to communicate the message of Jesus to your culture.

   Suggested Responses: Encourage participants to start thinking about what it actually means to go out into the world and be salt! Jesus commanded believers to go into all the world and to be "salt," which flavors everything around it. Help participants begin describing what that might look like.

SESSION TWO

The salt of the earth

Questions to think about

1. Describe the areas or ways in which you find it easy to compromise your faith and fit in with secular culture. What makes it difficult to stand up for Christ in these situations?

2. Describe the type of involvement in the secular world and with secular people that you as a Christian must have in order to communicate the message of Jesus to your culture.

3. Many of us have known Christians who seemed to be doing all the "right" spiritual things, yet compromised in one area and destroyed their testimony for God. What can we do to prevent such spiritual defeats?

PLANNING NOTES:

✏ **3.** Many of us have known Christians who seemed to be doing all the "right" spiritual things, yet compromised in one area and destroyed their testimony for God. What can we do to prevent such spiritual defeats?

Suggested Responses: We have to guard all aspects of our lives, we have to be watchful for attacks from the enemy, we have to be diligent and alert in our pursuit of godliness, we have to maintain our Christian identity, etc.

Let's keep these ideas in mind as we view the video.

video presentation
26 minutes

> *Participant's Guide page 38.*

On page 38 of your Participant's Guide, you will find space in which to take notes on key points as we watch this video.

Leader's Video Observations

John's Warning

The History of Sardis

Standing for God in a Pagan Culture

The Shops

The Synagogue

The Church

The Salt of the Earth

SESSION TWO

The Salt of the Earth

Questions to Think About

1. Describe the areas or ways in which you find it easy to compromise your faith and fit in with secular culture. What makes it difficult to stand up for Christ in these situations?

2. Describe the type of involvement in the secular world and with secular people that you as a Christian must have in order to communicate the message of Jesus to your culture.

3. Many of us have known Christians who seemed to be doing all the "right" spiritual things, yet compromised in one area and destroyed their testimony for God. What can we do to prevent such spiritual defeats?

Video Notes

John's Warning

The History of Sardis

Standing for God in a Pagan Culture
  The Shops

  The Synagogue

  The Church

The Salt of the Earth

group discovery

15 minutes

If your group has seven or more members, use the **Video Highlights** with the entire group (five minutes), then break into small groups of three to five to discuss the **Small Group Bible Discovery** (ten minutes).

If your group has fewer than seven members, begin with the **Video Highlights** (five minutes), then do one or more of the topics found in the **Small Group Bible Discovery** as a group (ten minutes).

Video Highlights (5 minutes)

Here you'll ask one or more of the following questions that directly relate to the video the participants have just seen.

1. What metaphor did John use to communicate his message to the church at Sardis? What was his message?

   Suggested Response: He used local history, particularly the mistake of Croesus, the Lydian king, to convey an essential message about the Christian walk. His message is that Christians cannot afford to become lazy or complacent. Satan needs only one overlooked area of our lives to severely damage our witness to a watching world.

Christian Church in the Temple of Artemis

2. What do the archaeological discoveries presented in this video tell you about the world-view of the religious Jews and Christians in Sardis?

   Suggested Responses: These will vary. Obviously their faith was important to them, they apparently wanted to make a public statement about their beliefs, they were very conscious of the culture around them, etc. We do not know, however, whether the synagogue in the gymnasium and the church in the temple represent a bold stand in a pagan culture or compromise with that culture.

   a. Which of these discoveries most surprised you? Why?

      Suggested Responses: These will vary but may include the large size of the synagogue and its location in the gymnasium, the number and significance of defaced pagan articles, etc.

video highlights

1. What metaphor did John use to communicate his message to the church at Sardis? What was his message?

Christian Church in the Temple of Artemis

2. What do the archaeological discoveries presented in this video tell you about the worldview of the religious Jews and Christians in Sardis?

   a. Which of these discoveries most surprised you? Why?

3. Which aspects of this video connected with you as you thought about your life and your culture? Why?

✏ **3.**   Which aspects of this video connected with you as you thought about your life and your culture? Why?

Suggested Responses: These will vary. Allow participants to share their concerns.

PROFILE OF A CITY

Sardis

- Stood in the middle of the Hermus River Valley, just over fifty miles east of the Mediterranean Sea in what's now the country of Turkey. The main east-west trade route came through this valley.
- On a spur of Mount Tmolus, on the north side of the Hermus River Valley, the Lydians—dominant people in the interior of Asia from about 1000–550 B.C.—built the acropolis of Sardis.
- The capital of the Lydians, Sardis enjoyed half a millennium of artistic, architectural, and economic prosperity. Its most famous king, Croesus, became rich because his subjects discovered a way to pan gold from a nearby river using sheep fleeces that trapped flecks of gold.
- When Nebuchadnezzar conquered Assyria, Sardis became part of his empire. In 586 B.C., he conquered Judah, destroyed Jerusalem and the temple, and exiled many Jews. Apparently many of them were brought to Sardis, and out of this community of Jews the church of Sardis was later born. It is amazing to see how God prepared things ahead of time for His purpose.
- The Persians made Sardis their western capital, so it remained an important city. Alexander the Great ended the Persian Empire in 334 B.C., and Sardis became part of the Greek world.

Sardis Trade Routes

40   Faith Lessons on the Early Church

2. What do the archaeological discoveries presented in this video tell you about the worldview of the religious Jews and Christians in Sardis?

     a. Which of these discoveries most surprised you? Why?

3. Which aspects of this video connected with you as you thought about your life and your culture? Why?

Session Two: The Salt of the Earth   41

PROFILE OF A CITY

Sardis

- Stood in the middle of the Hermus River Valley, just over fifty miles east of the Mediterranean Sea in what's now the country of Turkey. The main east-west trade route came through this valley.
- On a spur of Mount Tmolus, on the north side of the Hermus River Valley, the Lydians—dominant people in the interior of Asia from about 1000–550 B.C.—built the acropolis of Sardis.
- The capital of the Lydians, Sardis enjoyed half a millennium of artistic, architectural, and economic prosperity. Its most famous king, Croesus, became rich because his subjects discovered a way to pan gold from a nearby river using sheep fleeces that trapped flecks of gold.
- When Nebuchadnezzar conquered Assyria, Sardis became part of his empire. In 586 B.C., he conquered Judah, destroyed Jerusalem and the temple, and exiled many Jews. Apparently many of them were brought to Sardis, and out of this community of Jews the church of Sardis was later born. It is amazing to see how God prepared things ahead of time for His purpose.
- The Persians made Sardis their western capital, so it remained an important city. Alexander the Great ended the Persian Empire in 334 B.C., and Sardis became part of the Greek world.

Sardis Trade Routes

Small Group Bible Discovery (10 minutes)

> *Participant's Guide pages 42–55.*
>
> During this time, a group with fewer than seven participants will stay together. A group larger than seven participants will break into small groups. Assign each group one of the following topics. If you have more than five small groups, assign some topics to more than one group.

Let's break into groups of three to five—people sitting near you—and study some of the Bible passages and truths mentioned in the video.

Turn to pages 42–55 in your Participant's Guide. There you'll find a list of five topics. You'll have ten minutes to read and discuss the topic I'll assign to you.

> Assign each group a topic.

I'll signal you when one minute is left.

Topic A: "Be Salt"

On more than one occasion, Jesus told His followers that they were to be "salt" wherever they went. He also cautioned them not to lose their "saltiness." Let's investigate what this metaphor means to the Christian walk.

✏ 1. Where did Jesus want His disciples to demonstrate their faith? What did He want them to be? (See Matthew 5:13; Mark 16:15.)

Suggested Responses: They were to go into all the world and preach the good news to all of creation; they were the salt of the earth.

✏ 2. After seeing this video, describe in your own words what being the salt of the earth means.

Suggested Response: going into the world and mixing in with the evil of the world while demonstrating the good news without compromise or losing our Christian identity.

✏ 3. Jesus knew that being the salt of the earth would be a challenge. Note how He prays for His disciples in John 17:15–18.

a. What did Jesus ask for on behalf of His disciples as they lived out their faith in a pagan world? (See verse 15.)

Suggested Response: that God would protect them from Satan.

b. Which phrase did Jesus use to describe His disciples in verse 16? What do you think this means?

Suggested Responses: They were "not of the world." In other words, they were of the kingdom of heaven, just as Jesus was, and were called to live in the world in ways that glorified Him.

small Group Bible Discovery

Topic A: "Be Salt"

On more than one occasion, Jesus told His followers that they were to be "salt" wherever they went. He also cautioned them not to lose their "saltiness." Let's investigate what this metaphor means to the Christian walk.

1. Where did Jesus want His disciples to demonstrate their faith? What did He want them to be? (See Matthew 5:13; Mark 16:15.)

2. After seeing this video, describe in your own words what being the salt of the earth means.

3. Jesus knew that being the salt of the earth would be a challenge. Note how He prays for His disciples in John 17:15–18.

   a. What did Jesus ask for on behalf of His disciples as they lived out their faith in a pagan world? (See verse 15.)

   b. Which phrase did Jesus use to describe His disciples in verse 16? What do you think this means?

   c. To what did Jesus compare the disciples' ministry? (See verse 18.)

DID YOU KNOW?

Salt was very valuable during Jesus' day. It aided in the preservation of meat and enhanced the taste of food. But another less commonly known use of salt plays a key role in our understanding of what it means to be "salt" in our world.

During the first century, the people of Galilee used dome-shaped ovens made of hardened mud. Salt was mixed with dried dung—a common fuel—because the chemical reaction made the dung burn hotter and longer. Over time, however, the salt lost the qualities that made it effective. So, when it was no longer fit even for being mixed with manure, the "saltless" salt was thrown out.

Galilean Oven

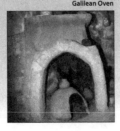

As believers, God calls us to "mix" with sinful people and yet keep our distinctive Christian identity. God sent His disciples into an evil world to live out the good news. They were not to lose their faith by absorbing the values of the pagan world, nor were they to be isolated from unbelievers.

c. To what did Jesus compare the disciples' ministry? (See verse 18.)

Suggested Response: Jesus had sent the disciples into the world, just as God the Father had sent Him into the world.

4. Read Matthew 5:13, Mark 9:50, and Luke 14:34–35. What thought is expressed in all three of these passages?

Suggested Response: Jesus warns His listeners not to lose their saltiness because once it is gone, it can't be made salty again and is good for nothing.

a. What can believers do to guard against losing their "saltiness"?

Suggested Responses: will vary but may include studying and keeping God's Word, constant prayer, seeking to be faithful to the truth of God in every way, being totally committed to Christ, etc.

DID YOU KNOW?

Salt was very valuable during Jesus' day. It aided in the preservation of meat and enhanced the taste of food. But another less commonly known use of salt plays a key role in our understanding of what it means to be "salt" in our world.

During the first century, the people of Galilee used dome-shaped ovens made of hardened mud. Salt was mixed with dried dung—a common fuel— because the chemical reaction made the dung burn hotter and longer. Over time, however, the salt lost the qualities that made it effective. So, when it was no longer fit even for being mixed with manure, the "saltless" salt was thrown out.

Galilean Oven

As believers, God calls us to "mix" with sinful people and yet keep our distinctive Christian identity. God sent His disciples into an evil world to live out the good news. They were not to lose their faith by absorbing the values of the pagan world, nor were they to be isolated from unbelievers.

b. Which phrase did Jesus use to describe His disciples in verse 16? What do you think this means?

c. To what did Jesus compare the disciples' ministry? (See verse 18.)

DID YOU KNOW?

Salt was very valuable during Jesus' day. It aided in the preservation of meat and enhanced the taste of food. But another less commonly known use of salt plays a key role in our understanding of what it means to be "salt" in our world.

During the first century, the people of Galilee used dome-shaped ovens made of hardened mud. Salt was mixed with dried dung—a common fuel—because the chemical reaction made the dung burn hotter and longer. Over time, however, the salt lost the qualities that made it effective.

So, when it was no longer fit even for being mixed with manure, the "saltless" salt was thrown out.

Galilean Oven

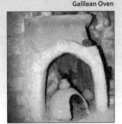

As believers, God calls us to "mix" with sinful people and yet keep our distinctive Christian identity. God sent His disciples into an evil world to live out the good news. They were not to lose their faith by absorbing the values of the pagan world, nor were they to be isolated from unbelievers.

4. Read Matthew 5:13, Mark 9:50, and Luke14:34–35. What thought is expressed in all three of these passages?

a. What can believers do to guard against losing their "saltiness"?

Topic B: John's Warning to the Church in Sardis

The history and archaeological discoveries made in Sardis provide valuable insights into the meaning and significance of the apostle John's warning to the church in that city.

1. Read Revelation 3:1–6 and answer the following questions, adding the appropriate historical or archaeological evidence.

a. What paradox existed concerning the church in Sardis? (See verse 1.)

b. What did John tell the Christians of Sardis to do? (See verse 2.)

Topic B: John's Warning to the Church in Sardis

The history and archaeological discoveries made in Sardis provide valuable insights into the meaning and significance of the apostle John's warning to the church in that city.

✏ 1. Read Revelation 3:1–6 and answer the following questions, adding the appropriate historical or archaeological evidence.

   a. What paradox existed concerning the church in Sardis? (See verse 1.)

   Suggested Response: The church had the reputation of being alive but was spiritually dead. (The church that was later built in the temple of Artemis may be an evidence of this.)

   b. What did John tell the Christians of Sardis to do? (See verse 2.)

   Suggested Response: He told them to wake up and strengthen what remained of their faith because they had not completed what God called them to do.

   c. Which specific steps toward reconciliation with God did John mention? (See verse 3.)

   Suggested Response: to remember what they had received and heard, to obey it, and to repent.

   d. Which consequences did John say would be forthcoming if they did not change their ways? (See verse 3.)

   Suggested Response: God would come like a "thief" without warning. (Perhaps alluding to the historical defeats of Sardis in the past.)

   e. According to verses 4–5, what do we learn about some of the Christians in Sardis? What hope did John promise to them and to others like them?

   Suggested Responses: Some had not compromised (perhaps the ones who displayed Christian symbols in their shops) and would walk with God. They would wear white clothing to illustrate their worthiness; their names would not be removed from the Book of Life; and their names would be acknowledged before God the Father and His angels.

WORTH OBSERVING . . .

An Unlearned Lesson

About 550 B.C., the Persians captured the acropolis of Sardis after a Persian soldier named Lagoras saw a soldier from Sardis climb down a steep, hidden trail to retrieve his helmet. Amazingly, a similar situation occurred in about 200 B.C.! A Greek soldier named Hyroeades watched a soldier of Sardis throw garbage off the top and noticed that vultures would wait on the wall until the garbage was thrown again. So, the Greeks realized that that portion of the wall was unguarded and captured the city by attacking that spot at night.

4. Read Matthew 5:13, Mark 9:50, and Luke 14:34–35. What thought is expressed in all three of these passages?

   a. What can believers do to guard against losing their "saltiness"?

Topic B: John's Warning to the Church in Sardis

The history and archaeological discoveries made in Sardis provide valuable insights into the meaning and significance of the apostle John's warning to the church in that city.

1. Read Revelation 3:1–6 and answer the following questions, adding the appropriate historical or archaeological evidence.

   a. What paradox existed concerning the church in Sardis? (See verse 1.)

   b. What did John tell the Christians of Sardis to do? (See verse 2.)

   c. Which specific steps toward reconciliation with God did John mention? (See verse 3.)

   d. Which consequences did John say would be forthcoming if they did not change their ways? (See verse 3.)

   e. According to verses 4–5, what do we learn about some of the Christians in Sardis? What hope did John promise to them and to others like them?

WORTH OBSERVING . . .

An Unlearned Lesson

About 550 B.C., the Persians captured the acropolis of Sardis after a Persian soldier named Lagoras saw a soldier from Sardis climb down a steep, hidden trail to retrieve his helmet. Amazingly, a similar situation occurred in about 200 B.C.! A Greek soldier named Hyroeades watched a soldier of Sardis throw garbage off the top and noticed that vultures would wait on the wall until the garbage was thrown again. So, the Greeks realized that that portion of the wall was unguarded and captured the city by attacking that spot at night.

Topic C: God's Strategy for the Early Missionaries

God has always intended for His people to live in the midst of culture and to influence it for Him. As they began to share the good news of Jesus with the world, the early missionaries went out from their home synagogues—the community center for Jewish life—and into the synagogues and cities of Asia Minor.

Roman Empire/Asia Minor

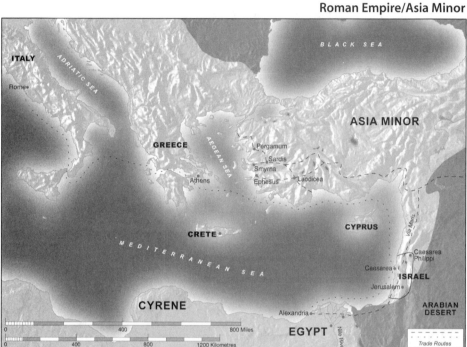

1. What was the "mission" of the Old Testament followers of God? (Read 1 Samuel 17:45–47; Isaiah 43:10–12.)

    Suggested Response: They were to be God's witnesses so that the whole world would know that there was a God in Israel.

2. What was the mission of the early Christian missionaries? (See Acts 1:8; 10:37–43.)

    Suggested Responses: to be God's witnesses in Jerusalem, Judea, Samaria, and to the ends of the earth and to be witnesses of everything Jesus had done and what had happened to Him.

3. Where had Jesus often taught His disciples, and what is significant about these locations? (Read Matthew 13:54; Mark 14:49.)

    Suggested Responses: Jesus taught in the temple courts and the synagogues, places where the people had the knowledge of God and His ways so that they could understand Jesus' message.

Topic C: God's Strategy for the Early Missionaries

God has always intended for His people to live in the midst of culture and to influence it for Him. As they began to share the good news of Jesus with the world, the early missionaries went out from their home synagogues—the community center for Jewish life—and into the synagogues and cities of Asia Minor.

1. What was the "mission" of the Old Testament followers of God? (Read 1 Samuel 17:45–47; Isaiah 43:10–12.)

Roman Empire/Asia Minor

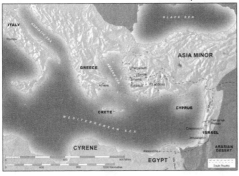

2. What was the mission of the early Christian missionaries? (See Acts 1:8; 10:37–43.)

3. Where had Jesus often taught His disciples, and what is significant about these locations? (Read Matthew 13:54; Mark 14:49.)

4. Read the following accounts of early Christian missionary efforts and note the strategy used.

Biblical Account	The Missionary Strategy
Acts 9:17–20	
Acts 13:1–5	
Acts 13:13–16	
Acts 14:1	
Acts 17:1–4	

✏ 4.   Read the following accounts of early Christian missionary efforts and note the strategy used.

Biblical Account	The Missionary Strategy
Acts 9:17–20	*Saul (Paul) preached in the synagogues of Damascus that Jesus was the Son of God.*
Acts 13:1–5	*Barnabas, Saul (Paul), and John proclaimed God's Word in the synagogues of Salamis.*
Acts 13:13–16	*Paul and his companions preached in the synagogue at Pisidian Antioch.*
Acts 14:1	*In Iconium Paul and Barnabas went "as usual" to the synagogue.*
Acts 17:1–4	*In Thessalonica, Paul, as was his custom, went into the local synagogue and reasoned with the people, proving that Jesus was the Christ. Some Jews and God-fearing Greeks were persuaded.*

DID YOU KNOW?

God Prepared Sardis to Receive the Good News

Jesus commanded His followers to "go into all the world and preach the good news to all creation" (Mark 16:15; Acts 1:8). It took His followers a while to understand the good news and what *all* the world meant, but as the Holy Spirit opened their hearts and minds, they began to go. Was the world prepared for them and their life-changing message? The answer is a resounding *yes!*

God had a specific strategy in mind for sending His message of salvation to the world. In Romans 1:16, Paul summarized it this way: "I am not ashamed of the gospel, because it is the power of God for the salvation of everyone who believes: *first* for the Jew, then for the Gentile [italics added]."

God commanded His people to reach the Jews first. Why? Because they were expecting the Messiah and were prepared to understand the gospel message because it involved the fulfillment of the Old Testament, which they knew. Also, God may have wanted Jews in each community to help Gentiles understand the roots of their newfound faith. So, when Paul, Silas, Barnabas, and other believers traveled to a new location, they went to the local synagogue and preached the news of Jesus Christ there. (See Acts 9:20; 13:5, 14; 14:1; 17:1–2, 10–12; 18:1–7, 19; 19:8.)

Although we don't know who started the church in Sardis, Jews were already living there when the early missionaries arrived with the gospel. In fact, hundreds of years before Jesus came to earth, God used pagan rulers to scatter Jewish populations across Asia Minor. For example, it is likely that Nebuchadnezzar of Babylon exiled Jews to Sardis when he destroyed Jerusalem in 586 B.C. Later, Cyrus of Persia encouraged more Jews to move to Asia Minor, and Antiochus—the pagan Greek king—brought two thousand Jewish families to Asia Minor during the third century, B.C.

Some of the descendants of these Jews were in Jerusalem during Pentecost (Acts 2:9), while others lived in cities such as Sardis—a key, influential city at the crossroads of the world. The Jewish presence in Asia Minor dramatically increased the impact and spread of the gospel. Truly God is in control of all things. All things work toward His plan (Romans 8:28), and God can use evil for good (see Genesis 50:20).

Today, God still does "advance" planning! Often He prepares the hearts of unbelievers so they'll be open to receiving the message of the Messiah. What's important is that we will be faithful to God's call and depend on Him to bring the spiritual fruit.

2. What was the mission of the early Christian missionaries? (See Acts 1:8; 10:37–43.)

3. Where had Jesus often taught His disciples, and what is significant about these locations? (Read Matthew 13:54; Mark 14:49.)

4. Read the following accounts of early Christian missionary efforts and note the strategy used.

Biblical Account	The Missionary Strategy
Acts 9:17–20	
Acts 13:1–5	
Acts 13:13–16	
Acts 14:1	
Acts 17:1–4	

DID YOU KNOW?

God Prepared Sardis to Receive the Good News

Jesus commanded His followers to "go into all the world and preach the good news to all creation" (Mark 16:15; Acts 1:8). It took His followers a while to understand the good news and what *all* the world meant, but as the Holy Spirit opened their hearts and minds, they began to go. Was the world prepared for them and their life-changing message? The answer is a resounding *yes!*

God had a specific strategy in mind for sending His message of salvation to the world. In Romans 1:16, Paul summarized it this way: "I am not ashamed of the gospel, because it is the power of God for the salvation of everyone who believes: *first* for the Jew, then for the Gentile [italics added]."

God commanded His people to reach the Jews first. Why? Because they were expecting the Messiah and were prepared to understand the gospel message because it involved the fulfillment of the Old Testament, which they knew. Also, God may have wanted Jews in each community to help Gentiles understand the roots of their newfound faith. So, when Paul, Silas, Barnabas, and other believers traveled to a new location, they went to the local synagogue and preached the news of Jesus Christ there. (See Acts 9:20; 13:5, 14; 14:1; 17:1–2, 10–12; 18:1–7, 19; 19:8.)

Although we don't know who started the church in Sardis, Jews were already living there when the early missionaries arrived with the gospel. In fact, hundreds of years before Jesus came to earth, God used pagan rulers to scatter Jewish populations across Asia Minor. For example, it is likely that Nebuchadnezzar of Babylon exiled Jews to Sardis when he destroyed Jerusalem in 586 B.C. Later, Cyrus of Persia encouraged more Jews to move to Asia Minor, and Antiochus—the pagan Greek king—brought two thousand Jewish families to Asia Minor during the third century, B.C.

Some of the descendants of these Jews were in Jerusalem during Pentecost (Acts 2:9), while others lived in cities such as Sardis—a key, influential city at the crossroads of the world. The Jewish presence in Asia Minor dramatically increased the impact and spread of the gospel. Truly

God is in control of all things. All things work toward His plan (Romans 8:28), and God can use evil for good (see Genesis 50:20).

Today, God still does "advance" planning! Often He prepares the hearts of unbelievers so they'll be open to receiving the message of the Messiah. What's important is that we will be faithful to God's call and depend on Him to bring the spiritual fruit.

Topic D: A God-Centered Versus a Human-Centered Worldview

As the early Christian missionaries began spreading Jesus' message, they encountered views of the world and of the nature of truth that differed greatly from their own. The conflict between a God-centered view of the world and a human-centered view of the world remains to this day—as it has since the Garden of Eden. Will people acknowledge God as the supreme being over all, or will they act as if they are the ultimate? Do human beings determine truth, or is God the source of all truth?

1. Who does the Bible teach is the ultimate, sovereign authority in the universe? (See Psalm 22:27–29; Isaiah 29:13–16; Romans 9:20–21.)

2. What was the underlying issue in Satan's tempting offer to Eve? (See Genesis 3:1–7.)

Topic D: A God-Centered Versus a Human-Centered Worldview

As the early Christian missionaries began spreading Jesus' message, they encountered views of the world and of the nature of truth that differed greatly from their own. The conflict between a God-centered view of the world and a human-centered view of the world remains to this day—as it has since the Garden of Eden. Will people acknowledge God as the supreme being over all, or will they act as if they are the ultimate? Do human beings determine truth, or is God the source of all truth?

1. Who does the Bible teach is the ultimate, sovereign authority in the universe? (See Psalm 22:27–29; Isaiah 29:13–16; Romans 9:20–21.)

    Suggested Responses: God is. He made us, He can confound human wisdom and intelligence at any time, He has dominion over all the earth.

2. What was the underlying issue in Satan's tempting offer to Eve? (See Genesis 3:1–7.)

    Suggested Responses: Satan offered her the chance to change her worldview, to be her own authority. She could "be like God, knowing good and evil"; she could gain power and control that only God had; she could take charge of her life and be a god in her own way; she had the right to determine her own actions; etc.

3. Hellenism, the dominant worldview in the first century, viewed human beings as ultimate in the universe, the human mind the source of the greatest wisdom, right and wrong a human choice, human accomplishment the goal of life, and the human body the greatest beauty. How does this worldview contrast with what Paul wrote concerning the Christian worldview? (See 1 Corinthians 1:18–25.)

    Suggested Responses: Whereas the Greeks sought human wisdom and declared themselves to be their own authority, Paul operated under the authority of God and power of Christ. He openly declared that the God he served could make fools of the wise philosophers and scholars and frustrate and destroy the world's wisdom. Furthermore, he proclaimed that even God's foolishness is wiser than man's wisdom and God's weakness is greater than man's strength.

4. Whose sovereignty did the believers declare to their world, and how did Satan respond? (See Acts 17:22–24; Jude 4–8.)

    Suggested Responses: The early believers declared the sovereignty of God, the Lord of heaven and earth who called them out of spiritual darkness. Satan used godless men to distort the truth of God and to encourage believers to commit immorality, deny Jesus Christ, reject authority, and "slander celestial beings."

5. What happens when people consider something or someone other than God to be the ultimate authority? (See Romans 1:18–32.)

    Suggested Responses: People who reject God earn His wrath, and He turns them over to be consumed by their own lusts—"futile" thinking, spiritually darkened and foolish hearts, sexual impurity, idolatry, and every kind of evil, greed, wickedness, depravity, etc.

God is in control of all things. All things work toward His plan (Romans 8:28), and God can use evil for good (see Genesis 50:20).

Today, God still does "advance" planning! Often He prepares the hearts of unbelievers so they'll be open to receiving the message of the Messiah. What's important is that we will be faithful to God's call and depend on Him to bring the spiritual fruit.

Topic D: A God-Centered Versus a Human-Centered Worldview

As the early Christian missionaries began spreading Jesus' message, they encountered views of the world and of the nature of truth that differed greatly from their own. The conflict between a God-centered view of the world and a human-centered view of the world remains to this day—as it has since the Garden of Eden. Will people acknowledge God as the supreme being over all, or will they act as if they are the ultimate? Do human beings determine truth, or is God the source of all truth?

1. Who does the Bible teach is the ultimate, sovereign authority in the universe? (See Psalm 22:27–29; Isaiah 29:13–16; Romans 9:20–21.)

2. What was the underlying issue in Satan's tempting offer to Eve? (See Genesis 3:1–7.)

3. Hellenism, the dominant worldview in the first century, viewed human beings as ultimate in the universe, the human mind the source of the greatest wisdom, right and wrong a human choice, human accomplishment the goal of life, and the human body the greatest beauty. How does this worldview contrast with what Paul wrote concerning the Christian worldview? (See 1 Corinthians 1:18–25.)

4. Whose sovereignty did the believers declare to their world, and how did Satan respond? (See Acts 17:22–24; Jude 4–8.)

5. What happens when people consider something or someone other than God to be the ultimate authority? (See Romans 1:18–32.)

A STUDY IN CONTRASTS

Hellenism, the dominant worldview in the first century, stands in stark contrast to the truths of God found in the Bible.

Hellenism	The Biblical Perspective
Human beings are the image of gods.	Only God is God, He is the Lord of the universe, the Creator of mankind.
The human mind is the greatest source of wisdom.	God is the ultimate source of all wisdom.
Human beings determine truth— what is right and wrong.	God, the source of truth, has given us the standards that determine what's right and wrong.
Human accomplishment is the goal of life.	The goal of life is to glorify and serve God.
The human body and what human beings create is the highest standard of beauty.	Human beings create beauty because they are made in the image of God.

DID YOU KNOW?

Jewish synagogues were more than just places to worship. They served as community centers for Jewish life. In the synagogue, the Jews prayed, taught school, held legal court, celebrated special times, and even lodged travelers. This may help us to understand why the synagogue in Sardis was located in the pagan gymnasium—the center of Jewish teaching was placed within the center of Hellenistic teaching.

Synagogue in Sardis

A STUDY IN CONTRASTS

Hellenism, the dominant worldview in the first century, stands in stark contrast to the truths of God found in the Bible.

Hellenism	The Biblical Perspective
Human beings are the image of gods.	Only God is God, He is the Lord of the universe, the Creator of mankind.
The human mind is the greatest source of wisdom.	God is the ultimate source of all wisdom.
Human beings determine truth—what is right and wrong.	God, the source of truth, has given us the standards that determine what's right and wrong.
Human accomplishment is the goal of life.	The goal of life is to glorify and serve God.
The human body and what human beings create is the highest standard of beauty.	Human beings create beauty because they are made in the image of God.

DID YOU KNOW?

Jewish synagogues were more than just places to worship. They served as community centers for Jewish life. In the synagogue, the Jews prayed, taught school, held legal court, celebrated special times, and even lodged travelers. This may help us to understand why the synagogue in Sardis was located in the pagan gymnasium—the center of Jewish teaching was placed within the center of Hellenistic teaching.

Synagogue in Sardis

DATA FILE

The Greek Gymnasium

Every major Hellenistic city had an educational institution called a gymnasium, in which citizens of the Greek/Roman community were taught the wisdom of Hellenism. Religious Jews during biblical times believed the gymnasium to be an abomination because education there was based on the view that humans are the ultimate source of truth, many activities were done naked, and students had to make certain pagan religious commitments in order to participate.

Several passages in Paul's writings imply that he was aware of gymnasiums: 1 Timothy 4:8 includes the expression "physical training" that is based on the Greek word for *gymnasium*; 1 Corinthians 9:24–27 mentions competitions such as boxing and running; and Galatians 2:2; 5:7 and Philippians 2:16 mention running. In Galatians 3:24, Paul also used

Gymnasium of Sardis

the Greek word *paidagogos,* which referred to the slave attendant who accompanied students from wealthy families to school in order to tutor them in the lessons they received from the teacher in the gymnasium.

Features of the Gymnasium at Sardis

The Palaestra

In this large (six hundred by one hundred fifty feet) open area to the east of the Marble Court, physical education was done on the sand floor. Smaller rooms around the outside were also used for physical training—conditioning (weights and calisthenics), skill development (discus, javelin, jumping), and cardiovascular training (running). Also in these rooms the students relaxed with massage and oil treatments after their exercise and classroom learning.

The Didaskelion

Located on the outside of the open area, this school for academics provided rooms in which students learned and recited lessons. There were three levels of education: elementary (boys and girls ages five to twelve who studied reading and writing); secondary (boys and girls ages twelve to sixteen who studied philosophy, math, science, and music); and advanced (boys ages sixteen through adulthood who studied philosophy, medicine, music, and science).

The Marble Court

This three-story, colonnaded courtyard was dedicated to the cult of the Roman emperor—believed to be the guardian of the truth being taught and exemplified in his life. All learning was devoted to him. Many niches in the walls served as pediments for statues. In the main apse was a statue of the emperor, who was honored with sacrifices and ceremonies during the educational process.

DATA FILE

The Greek Gymnasium

Every major Hellenistic city had an educational institution called a gymnasium, in which citizens of the Greek/Roman community were taught the wisdom of Hellenism. Religious Jews during biblical times believed the gymnasium to be an abomination because education there was based on the view that humans are the ultimate source of truth, many activities were done naked, and students had to make certain pagan religious commitments in order to participate.

Gymnasium of Sardis

Several passages in Paul's writings imply that he was aware of gymnasiums: 1 Timothy 4:8 includes the expression "physical training" that is based on the Greek word for *gymnasium*; 1 Corinthians 9:24–27 mentions competitions such as boxing and running; and Galatians 2:2; 5:7 and Philippians 2:16 mention running. In Galatians 3:24, Paul also used the Greek word *paidagogos*, which referred to the slave attendant who accompanied students from wealthy families to school in order to tutor them in the lessons they received from the teacher in the gymnasium.

Features of the Gymnasium at Sardis

The Palaestra

In this large (six hundred by one hundred fifty feet), open area to the east of the Marble Court, physical education was done on the sand floor. Smaller rooms around the outside were also used for physical training—conditioning (weights and calisthenics), skill development (discus, javelin, jumping), and cardiovascular training (running). Also in these rooms the students relaxed with massage and oil treatments after their exercise and classroom learning.

The Didaskelion

Located on the outside of the open area, this school for academics provided rooms in which students learned and recited lessons. There were three levels of education: elementary (boys and girls ages five to twelve who studied reading and writing); secondary (boys and girls ages twelve to sixteen who studied philosophy, math, science, and music); and advanced (boys ages sixteen through adulthood who studied philosophy, medicine, music and science).

The Marble Court

This three-story, colonnaded courtyard was dedicated to the cult of the Roman emperor—believed to be the guardian of the truth being taught and exemplified in his life. All learning was devoted to him. Many niches in the walls served as pediments for statues. In the main apse was a statue of the emperor, who was honored with sacrifices and ceremonies during the educational process.

The Bath Complex

In the western section was the largest pool, the heated caldarium. East of this was a large, central hall and the warm pool (tepidarium). A nearby oblong hall held the cold pool (frigidarium) where students completed their bathing. There were also fountains in niches in the walls.

The Synagogue

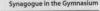

Synagogue in the Gymnasium

Holding more than one thousand people (estimated), this is the largest synagogue ever found in the ancient world. It was not part of the original gymnasium and was added later, just after the time of the New Testament. Here, impressive mosaic floors added to the beauty of the structure and testify to the community's wealth. More than eighty inscriptions have been found in the synagogue that indicate that some Jews had significant status and wealth in Sardis and that others were Gentile converts.

The Bath Complex

In the western section was the largest pool, the heated caldarium. East of this was a large, central hall and the warm pool (tepidarium). A nearby oblong hall held the cold pool (frigidarium) where students completed their bathing. There were also fountains in niches in the walls.

The Synagogue

Holding more than one thousand people (estimated), this is the largest synagogue ever found in the ancient world. It was not part of the original gymnasium and was added later, just after the time of the New Testament. Here, impressive mosaic floors added to the beauty of the structure and testify to the community's wealth. More than eighty inscriptions have been found in the synagogue that indicate that some Jews had significant status and wealth in Sardis and that others were Gentile converts.

Synagogue in the Gymnasium

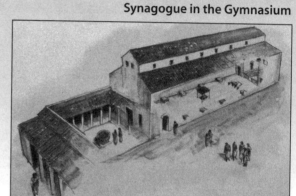

Topic E: Standing for God in a Pagan World

Standing for God within an evil culture is something every individual follower of Christ is called to do. By studying what other followers of God have done to display their faith, we can learn more about displaying our faith to our world.

1. How did God describe the nature of pagan worship among Israel's neighbors during Old Testament times? (See Exodus 34:15–16.)

    Suggested Responses: They prostituted themselves to their gods and sacrificed to them, and God warned the Israelites that they would entice Israel to do the same.

2. How did Paul describe the pagan world of his day, which would have included the city of Sardis? (See Romans 1:18–26.)

    Suggested Responses: Pagan people had exchanged the truth of God for a lie and chose to serve created things rather than God who created them. They were godless, wicked, and suppressed the truth. They disregarded the proofs they had of God and refused to glorify Him, preferring to worship false images and degrade themselves through sexual immorality.

3. Where did Jesus intend for His followers to live out their faith? What did He desire for them? (See John 17:15–19.)

    Suggested Responses: in the world. But He did not want them to be of the world, He wanted them to be protected from the evil one, to go out into the world as He had gone into it, and that they would remain faithful.

The Didaskelion

Located on the outside of the open area, this school for academics provided rooms in which students learned and recited lessons. There were three levels of education: elementary (boys and girls ages five to twelve who studied reading and writing); secondary (boys and girls ages twelve to sixteen who studied philosophy, math, science, and music); and advanced (boys ages sixteen through adulthood who studied philosophy, medicine, music and science).

The Marble Court

This three-story, colonnaded courtyard was dedicated to the cult of the Roman emperor—believed to be the guardian of the truth being taught and exemplified in his life. All learning was devoted to him. Many niches in the walls served as pediments for statues. In the main apse was a statue of the emperor, who was honored with sacrifices and ceremonies during the educational process.

The Bath Complex

In the western section was the largest pool, the heated caldarium. East of this was a large, central hall and the warm pool (tepidarium). A nearby oblong hall held the cold pool (frigidarium) where students completed their bathing. There were also fountains in niches in the walls.

The Synagogue

Holding more than one thousand people (estimated), this is the largest synagogue ever found in the ancient world. It was not part of the original gymnasium and was added later, just after the time of the New Testament. Here, impressive mosaic floors added to the beauty of the structure and testify to the community's wealth. More than eighty inscriptions have been found in the synagogue that indicate that some Jews had significant status and wealth in Sardis and that others were Gentile converts.

Synagogue in the Gymnasium

Topic E: Standing for God in a Pagan World

Standing for God within an evil culture is something every individual follower of Christ is called to do. By studying what other followers of God have done to display their faith, we can learn more about displaying our faith to our world.

1. How did God describe the nature of pagan worship among Israel's neighbors during Old Testament times? (See Exodus 34:15–16.)

2. How did Paul describe the pagan world of his day, which would have included the city of Sardis? (See Romans 1:18–26.)

3. Where did Jesus intend for His followers to live out their faith? What did He desire for them? (See John 17:15–19.)

4. Where was Paul committed to proclaim his faith? What freedom did he claim? (See 1 Corinthians 9:19–23.)

✏ 4. Where was Paul committed to proclaim his faith? What freedom did he claim? (See 1 Corinthians 9:19–23.)

Suggested Responses: Paul was committed to proclaim his faith wherever and to whomever would listen. He claimed the freedom to do whatever was necessary to identify with different people in order to lead as many of them to Jesus as he could.

✏ 5. What "freedom" did Christians who had lived pagan lifestyles not have? (Read 1 Corinthians 5:9–11.)

Suggested Responses: They did not have the freedom to continue in lawless, immoral, and idolatrous living. In fact, believers were to disassociate themselves from any believers who persisted in living a pagan lifestyle.

> Signal the groups when one minute remains so that they may wrap up their discovery time.

Faith Lesson

7 minutes

Time for Reflection (4 minutes)

It's time for each of us to think quietly about how we can be "salt" in our world. On page 55 of the Participant's Guide, you'll find a passage of Scripture. Let's each read this passage silently and take the next few minutes to consider some of the questions that follow the Scripture passage.

Please do not talk during this time. It's a time when we all can reflect on today's lesson and how it applies to our lives.

> The Scripture passage and questions are reproduced in their entirety in the Participant's Guide on pages 55–56.

But you are a chosen people, a royal priesthood, a holy nation, a people belonging to God, that you may declare the praises of him who called you out of darkness into his wonderful light. Once you were not a people, but now you are the people of God; once you had not received mercy, but now you have received mercy.

Dear friends, I urge you, as aliens and strangers in the world, to abstain from sinful desires, which war against your soul. Live such good lives among the pagans that, though they accuse you of doing wrong, they may see your good deeds and glorify God on the day he visits us. (1 Peter 2:9–12)

Consider the ways in which Peter's words:

- stand in contrast to the pagan worldview
- remind believers that they are to be in the world but not of it
- encourage obedience to God's commands
- reinforce the concept that they are God's witnesses to a pagan world.

Imagine that Peter wrote these words directly to you:

- In what ways can you declare God's praises?
- What are the sinful desires that wage war against your soul?

Topic E: Standing for God in a Pagan World

Standing for God within an evil culture is something every individual follower of Christ is called to do. By studying what other followers of God have done to display their faith, we can learn more about displaying our faith to our world.

1. How did God describe the nature of pagan worship among Israel's neighbors during Old Testament times? (See Exodus 34:15–16.)

2. How did Paul describe the pagan world of his day, which would have included the city of Sardis? (See Romans 1:18–26.)

3. Where did Jesus intend for His followers to live out their faith? What did He desire for them? (See John 17:15–19.)

4. Where was Paul committed to proclaim his faith? What freedom did he claim? (See 1 Corinthians 9:19–23.)

5. What "freedom" did Christians who had lived pagan lifestyles not have? (Read 1 Corinthians 5:9–11.)

faith lesson

Time for Reflection

Read the following passage of Scripture and take the next few minutes to consider the ways in which you can be "salt" in your world.

> But you are a chosen people, a royal priesthood, a holy nation, a people belonging to God, that you may declare the praises of him who called you out of darkness into his wonderful light. Once you were not a people, but now you are the people of God; once you had not received mercy, but now you have received mercy.
>
> Dear friends, I urge you, as aliens and strangers in the world, to abstain from sinful desires, which war against your soul. Live such good lives among the pagans that, though they accuse you of doing wrong, they may see your good deeds and glorify God on the day he visits us.
>
> 1 PETER 2:9–12

Consider the ways in which Peter's words:

- stand in contrast to the pagan worldview
- remind believers that they are to be in the world but not of it
- encourage obedience to God's commands
- reinforce the concept that they are God's witnesses to a pagan world.

Imagine that Peter wrote these words directly to you:

- In what ways can you declare God's praises?
- What are the sinful desires that wage war against your soul?

- In which aspects of life are you so committed to God's worldview that you seem to be a stranger in the world?
- In what ways can you live such a good life that people who do not know God take notice and glorify God?

Action Points (3 minutes)

> The following points are reproduced on pages 56–58 of the Participant's Guide:

Now it's time to wrap up our session.

> Give participants a moment to transition from their thoughtfulness to giving you their full attention.

I'd like to take a moment to summarize the key points we explored. After I have reviewed these points, I will give you a moment to jot down an action step (or steps) that you will commit to this week as a result of what you have learned today.

> Read the following points and pause afterward so that participants can consider and write out their commitment.

1. *Jesus sent His disciples out to be "salt" in an evil world.* They were to go into the world and live out the good news without compromise. They were to retain their distinctiveness without isolating themselves from unbelievers.

   The evidence of Sardis raises the question of whether the Jews and Christians of that city were a distinctive influence among their pagan neighbors or whether they compromised their calling and lost the distinctive beliefs and lifestyle that are essential to faith in God.

   Consider the ways in which you are being "salt" in the world and consider also the ways in which you may be avoiding the world and therefore are missing opportunities to share Jesus' message. Write down specific examples of both.

I am "salt" in an evil world:	I am avoiding the world:

As you consider the world in which you live, where in your community do you need to step out of your comfort zone and be "salt"?

- In which aspects of life are you so committed to God's world-view that you seem to be a stranger in the world?
- In what ways can you live such a good life that people who do not know God take notice and glorify God?

Action Points

Take a moment to jot down an action step (or steps) that you will commit to this week as a result of what you have learned.

1. *Jesus sent His disciples out to be "salt" in an evil world.* They were to go into the world and live out the good news without compromise. They were to retain their distinctiveness without isolating themselves from unbelievers.

   The evidence of Sardis raises the question of whether the Jews and Christians of that city were a distinctive influence among their pagan neighbors or whether they compromised their calling and lost the distinctive beliefs and lifestyle that are essential to faith in God.

   Consider the ways in which you are being "salt" in the world and consider also the ways in which you may be avoiding the world and therefore are missing opportunities to share Jesus' message. Write down specific examples of both.

I am "salt" in an evil world:	I am avoiding the world:

PLANNING NOTES:

✏ 2. *John used a well-known, local, historical metaphor when he warned the Christians of Sardis to influence their world without compromising with it.* "I know your deeds," he wrote, "you have a reputation of being alive, but you are dead. Wake up! . . . but if you do not wake up, I will come like a thief, and you will not know at what time I will come to you" (Revelation 3:1–3).

This reminder applies to Christians today as well. We must be careful to stay watchful, alert, and alive to what's going on in our Christian walk. Otherwise, we might become apathetic or make a mistake that would cause our witness to a watching world to collapse.

In what way(s) have you—even in small ways—compromised your faith? Note particularly the ways in which you have become careless or apathetic toward your Christian calling.

Which particular sin(s) do you need to repent of in order to straighten out your relationship with God? Be specific.

✏ 3. *Worldview is important.* The Greeks in Sardis taught Hellenism, which glorified human beings and considered them to be the center of the universe, the source of all wisdom. This view stands in opposition to the biblical worldview that recognizes God as Lord of the universe and the source of all truth.

The great spiritual struggle throughout human history has been whether or not people choose to recognize God as the supreme being or insist on declaring themselves as the ultimate being.

In what ways are you tempted to adopt a more human-centered worldview? Be specific.

I, _____, realize that my commitment to recognize God as Lord of the universe and as the supreme authority in my life needs to be strengthened. I want God to be at the center of my universe. In order to have a more God-centered worldview, I will _____

_____.

closing prayer
I minute

In this session, we have been challenged to retain our distinctiveness as Christians while at the same time living among unbelievers. Let's pray now and ask God to guide and strengthen us as we seek to be "salt" among people who have not yet accepted Jesus as their Lord and Savior.

Dear God, it's hard to be in the world and yet not conform to its values. Yet we truly want to share Your message and live in ways that honor You and draw people to You. Please make us more mindful of the work of Your Holy Spirit in our lives. Help us to be ever watchful to guard against complacency and sin in our walk with You. Empower us to share Your truth in the "tough" places in our community and to remain faithful to You. Guide and protect us as we take Your message into the gymnasiums of our culture. In Jesus' name we pray. Amen.

As you consider the world in which you live, where in your community do you need to step out of your comfort zone and be "salt"?

2. *John used a well-known, local, historical metaphor when he warned the Christians of Sardis to influence their world without compromising with it.* "I know your deeds," he wrote, "you have a reputation of being alive, but you are dead. Wake up!... but if you do not wake up, I will come like a thief, and you will not know at what time I will come to you" (Revelation 3:1–3).

This reminder applies to Christians today as well. We must be careful to stay watchful, alert, and alive to what's going on in our Christian walk. Otherwise, we might become apathetic or make a mistake that would cause our witness to a watching world to collapse.

In what way(s) have you—even in small ways—compromised your faith? Note particularly the ways in which you have become careless or apathetic toward your Christian calling.

Which particular sin(s) do you need to repent of in order to straighten out your relationship with God? Be specific.

3. *Worldview is important.* The Greeks in Sardis taught Hellenism, which glorified human beings and considered them to be the center of the universe, the source of all wisdom. This view stands in opposition to the biblical worldview that recognizes God as Lord of the universe and the source of all truth.

The great spiritual struggle throughout human history has been whether or not people choose to recognize God as the supreme being or insist on declaring themselves as the ultimate being.

In what ways are you tempted to adopt a more human-centered worldview? Be specific.

I, _____, realize that my commitment to recognize God as Lord of the universe and as the supreme authority in my life needs to be strengthened. I want God to be at the center of my universe. In order to have a more God-centered worldview, I will _____

_____

_____.

where satan lives

before you lead

Synopsis

The apostle John wrote a letter to the Christians who lived in Pergamum, which was for a time the capital and one of the largest cities in the Roman province of Asia Minor. Recorded in Revelation 2:12–17, this letter is identified as being "the words of him who has the sharp, double-edged sword" (verse 12). As Ray Vander Laan points out, this introduction held special significance for the people of Pergamum. The provincial governor in that city had what was known as "the right of the sword"—Rome's authority to decide which prisoners or accused persons would live or die (including Christians who refused to honor the "divine" Caesar). So John's letter is a clear statement that Jesus—not the Roman governor—has power over life and death.

John also gives the city of Pergamum an unusual designation: "I know where you live—where Satan has his throne. Yet you remain true to my name. You did not renounce your faith in me, even in the days of Antipas, my faithful witness, who was put to death in your city—where Satan lives" (verse 13).

In this session, we'll explore possible reasons why John referred to Pergamum as the place where Satan lived and what it was like for believers to live there. Consider some of the possibilities:

- A beautiful temple dedicated to the god, Dionysus, stood prominently on the Acropolis. Believed to be the son of Zeus and a human mother, Dionysus supposedly offered his followers life after death and meaningful life on earth through indulgence in raw meat and wine. According to the teachings of the Dionysus cult, followers who drank wine to excess literally became one with Dionysus. So, worshipers would gather around the altar, gorge on raw meat that had been offered to Dionysus, and drink until they became intoxicated. During the festivals, women would drink wine and run through the hills screaming, dancing, and committing sexual immorality. Dionysus worship was so wild that it was outlawed in Rome because it was considered to be too immoral!

  As Ray points out, Jesus had prepared His disciples well for the cults they would encounter as they took the gospel throughout the world. Concerning the claims of Dionysus, for example, John could say, "Dionysus is a counterfeit. Jesus was born of God through a woman. I watched Him turn water into wine (the same miracle that Dionysus supposedly performed in secret in his temples at night). Only Jesus can provide meaning and true intimacy with God. I've seen that firsthand."

- When the people of Pergamum needed healing, they went to the temple shrine of Asclepius—the snake god of healing. Everyone who entered the hospital complex passed a snake symbol and thereby credited any healing they would receive to the snake god. Priests interviewed potential patients to determine whether they were acceptable for healing. Interestingly, they turned away people who were dying and women who were ready to deliver babies. They didn't want a patient's death to "taint" their god.

  Once accepted, patients were led through an underground tunnel to a huge treatment room where they went to sleep, probably after being drugged. The patients waited to receive a vision of treatment from Asclepius, which they would reveal to the priests, who in turn would prescribe treatment(s). The main treatments related to water, so patients would take mud baths or drink sacred spring water. Exercise, dietary changes, rest, and attending the theater were also prescribed. Once healed, patients bowed down on their knees before a statue of Asclepius, thanked him for their healing, and gave him gifts. Finally, they would inscribe their name and the ailment from which they had been cured on a large, white stone as a testimony to the god.

  During His ministry on earth, Jesus had provided John and the other disciples with evidence that refuted the claims of this god. Jews and Christians already knew that the snake, the symbol of Asclepius, symbolized evil in the Garden of Eden and represented everything sinful and Satanic. Furthermore, the second and third miracles recorded in John's Gospel have to do with Jesus' power to heal. Jesus raised a dead child and healed a man who had been waiting for thirty-eight years to be healed at the Pool of Bethesda (near what some scholars believe was an Asclepius temple). John actually had seen Jesus heal people, something no "snake" god could do.

- The shrine of Demeter, the goddess of grain who supposedly provided food, was popular among the common people of Pergamum. She also was said to forgive the sins of her followers who immersed themselves in bulls' blood.

  John was prepared to counter these counterfeit blessings as well. Having seen Jesus the Messiah feed five thousand people using a few loaves and fishes, John knew that Jesus, not Demeter, put groceries on the table. John also knew that Jesus was the only one who could take away people's sins through the blood He shed on the cross.

- Pergamum was the first city to establish an emperor cult. People worshiped the Roman emperor, Caesar Augustus, at the Athena temple.

  As one of the disciples who had stood on the Mount of Olives and watched Jesus ascend to heaven, John knew beyond a doubt that Jesus, not Caesar Augustus or any other emperor, was seated at the right hand of God.

  In Pergamum, as in our culture today, Satan wanted people to lose sight of God and His power. All of the false gods who usurped the credit God deserves for providing life and giving it meaning and significance made Pergamum the city "where Satan lived." Satan wanted people to think that everything they needed for life—even eternal life—could be found through their own efforts or through the world around them.

With the background of Pergamum, the place where Satan lived, in mind, Ray focuses on John's closing words to the church in Pergamum: "I will also give him a white stone with a new name written on it, known only to him who receives it." God strategically placed the early believers in an evil world to stand as testimonies to His power and work in their lives. As standing stones for God, they were clearly different from the white stones on which people healed by Asclepius had written their names. The world needed to see the believers as white stones on which new names had been written, and the believers needed to speak the truth of God to a spiritually hungry world. Likewise, believers today need to praise God for all that He has done and tell other people about it.

Key Points of This Lesson

1. *The host of pagan gods worshiped in Pergamum encouraged people to seek what they needed for life somewhere other than from God. Perhaps that's why John wrote that Satan "lived" in that city, which was noted for its many shrines and temples.*

   People were drawn to the wine drinking and sexual license as well as the promise of physical healing, provision of food, forgiveness of sins, and immortality. Clearly Satan wanted people to believe that meaning and significance—even eternal life—could be found through themselves, false gods, or the world around them. Satan still offers this temptation to people today.

2. *Having been carefully prepared ahead of time by Jesus, John and the other early missionaries knew the truth about Satan's counterfeit blessings.* They knew that God and God alone is the source of all true blessings. John had witnessed Jesus' life and miracles firsthand and was prepared to refute the claims of false religions.

3. *Using the imagery of the white stones inscribed by people who supposedly had been healed by Asclepius, John challenged believers in Pergamum to stand courageously as witnesses for God, telling what He had done in their lives and giving Him the credit He was due.*

   Believers today have the important responsibility of expressing God's truth to a spiritually hungry world. We need to let people know what God has done for us and praise God for all that He has done—the "ordinary" as well as the extraordinary.

Session Outline (55 minutes)

    I. Introduction (5 minutes)
       Welcome
       What's to Come
       Questions to Think About

    II. Show Video "Where Satan Lives" (25 minutes)

    III. Group Discovery (15 minutes)
       Video Highlights
       Small Group Bible Discovery

    IV. Faith Lesson (9 minutes)
       Time for Reflection
       Action Points

    V. Closing Prayer (1 minute)

Materials

No additional materials are needed for this session. Simply view the video prior to leading the session so you are familiar with its main points.

where satan lives

introduction

5 minutes

Welcome

> Assemble the participants together and welcome them to session three of *Faith Lessons on the Early Church*.

What's to Come

Pergamum, at one time the capital city of the Roman province of Asia Minor, was known for its spectacular architecture and many beautiful temples dedicated to a variety of gods. Yet, in Revelation 2, the apostle John describes Pergamum as being "where Satan has his throne" and "where Satan lives." This session focuses on the many candidates that would make Pergamum Satan's throne and how Jesus had prepared His disciples to boldly confront these evils. It also draws our attention to the small but influential group of Christians in Pergamum who remained faithful to God.

Questions to Think About

> *Participant's Guide page* 59.
>
> Ask each question and solicit a few responses from group members.

1. What are some of the ways in which people today try to find meaning and significance on their own, without God?

   Suggested Responses: seek the security and pleasure of material possessions, strive to attain fame, take up various causes to "do good," turn to physical relationships to find intimacy, try different religions, etc.

2. In what ways do people—even Christians—take credit for things that God has done? List subtle as well as obvious ways.

   Suggested Responses: Encourage participants to open their eyes to all that God actually does for us. May include taking credit for accumulating wealth, believing that good health comes from our own efforts, believing that our skills or abilities are anything other than a gift from God, etc.

SESSION THREE

where satan lives

questions to think about

1. What are some of the ways in which people today try to find meaning and significance on their own, without God?

2. In what ways do people—even Christians—take credit for things that God has done? List subtle as well as obvious ways.

3. When you are trying to follow God but people around you are pursuing other directions, what enables you to persevere in your faith even when the pressure mounts to go along with others?

PLANNING NOTES:

✏ 3.   When you are trying to follow God but people around you are pursuing other directions, what enables you to persevere in your faith even when the pressure mounts to go along with others?

Suggested Responses: These will vary. Encourage participants to describe specifically their "anchor point" for following God, which may include spending time with other Christians, a daily time of prayer and Bible study, recalling what God has done for them, praising God, etc.

Let's keep these ideas in mind as we view the video.

video presentation
25 minutes

Participant's Guide page 60.

On page 60 of your Participant's Guide, you will find a space in which to take notes on key points as we watch this video.

Leader's Video Observations

The City of Pergamum—Where Satan Has His Throne

The Temples of Counterfeit Gods

Dionysus

Asclepius

Demeter

Others

The True Source of Meaning in Life

SESSION THREE

where satan lives

questions to think about

1. What are some of the ways in which people today try to find meaning and significance on their own, without God?

2. In what ways do people—even Christians—take credit for things that God has done? List subtle as well as obvious ways.

3. When you are trying to follow God but people around you are pursuing other directions, what enables you to persevere in your faith even when the pressure mounts to go along with others?

video notes

The City of Pergamum—Where Satan Has His Throne

The Temples of Counterfeit Gods

    Dionysus

    Asclepius

    Demeter

    Others

The True Source of Meaning in Life

PLANNING NOTES:

group Discovery

I5 minutes

> If your group has seven or more members, use the **Video Highlights** with the entire group (5 minutes), then break into small groups of three to five to discuss the **Small Group Bible Discovery** (10 minutes).
>
> If your group has fewer than seven members, begin with the **Video Highlights** (5 minutes), then do one or more of the topics found in the **Small Group Bible Discovery** as a group (10 minutes).

Video Highlights (5 minutes)

> Here you'll ask one or more of the following questions that directly relate to the video the participants have just seen.

1. Were you surprised to discover the ways in which Satan "counterfeited" the claims of Jesus in Pergamum? Why or why not?

    Suggested Responses: These will vary. Encourage participants to consider how clever Satan is in luring people away from God—how well Satan knows human needs and desires, how well Satan knows what God really offers and how closely he will imitate it.

2. How would you define what John meant by "Satan's throne" and the place "where Satan lives"?

    Suggested Responses: Encourage participants to envision the "big picture." Where Satan lives isn't a particular temple or cult; it is anything that robs God of His rightful authority or the credit He deserves. Thus any form of idolatry robs God of His proper authority and denies Him the credit for what He provides.

3. What parallels do you see between the worship of the various gods of Pergamum and our own culture? In what ways can these activities and beliefs in our culture be identified as the place "where Satan lives"?

    Suggested Responses: Encourage participants to see how very little things have changed. For example, as in the Dionysus cult, there are still groups that promote immoral and even self-destructive behavior as a type of "worship." The desire to create one's own physical healing or good health through diet, exercise, healing mud and water, herbs, and the like is very popular today—and God rarely (if ever) receives credit for it.

4. Describe what you think it was like to live as a Christian in Pergamum.

    Suggested Responses: will vary. Encourage participants to consider the difficult as well as the exciting and inspiring. Difficult because of the evil around them—the worship of false gods, the "right of the sword," because Christians were martyred there, etc. Exciting because of the opportunity to stand for Jesus—to see God at work, to know His truth, etc.

video highlights

1. Were you surprised to discover the ways in which Satan "counterfeited" the claims of Jesus in Pergamum? Why or why not?

2. How would you define what John meant by "Satan's throne" and the place "where Satan lives"?

3. What parallels do you see between the worship of the various gods of Pergamum and our own culture? In what ways can these activities and beliefs in our culture be identified as the place "where Satan lives"?

4. Describe what you think it was like to live as a Christian in Pergamum.

PLANNING NOTES:

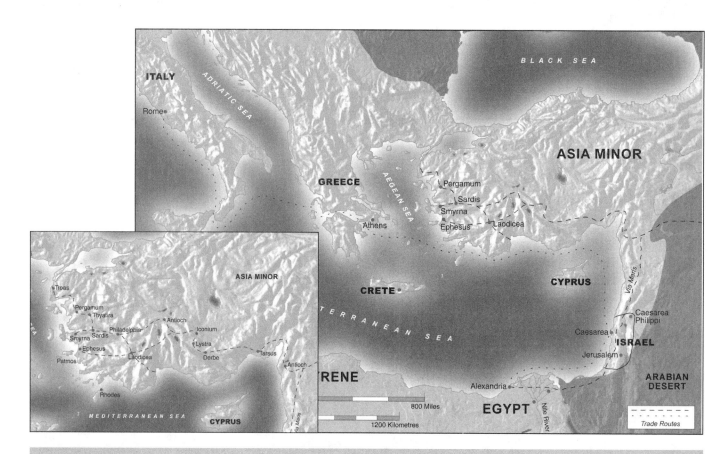

PROFILE OF A CITY

Pergamum

Pergamum (now Bergama) is located in the northern part of the Roman province of Asia Minor, along the Caicus River about ten miles from the Aegean Sea. From the third century B.C. until well into the fourth century A.D., its kings controlled a major trade road from the East (Persia) to the Mediterranean world.

Following the city's conquest by Alexander the Great in 334 B.C., its strategic location was recognized by Lysimachos, who turned it into a military base. From that point on, it became an increasingly significant Hellenistic city—rich in culture, spectacular in architecture, and powerful in its worship of pagan gods.

Its last king, Attalos III, willed the city to the Roman Empire so that its glory would not be spoiled by war. This proved to be a wise move because the Romans respected its cultural glory and religious character, making Pergamum the capital of the province of Asia Minor for a period of time. The Romans also left their mark on the city when it became the first city in which the cult of "divine" Caesars was established.

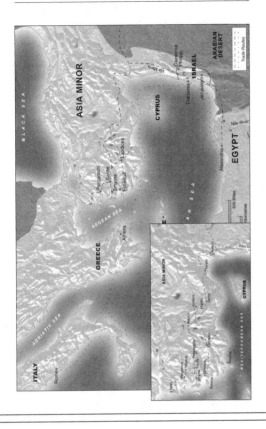

PROFILE OF A CITY

Pergamum

Pergamum (now Bergama) is located in the northern part of the Roman province of Asia Minor, along the Caicus River about ten miles from the Aegean Sea. From the third century B.C. until well into the fourth century A.D., its kings controlled a major trade road from the East (Persia) to the Mediterranean world.

Following the city's conquest by Alexander the Great in 334 B.C., its strategic location was recognized by Lysimachos, who turned it into a military base. From that point on, it became an increasingly significant Hellenistic city—rich in culture, spectacular in architecture, and powerful in its worship of pagan gods.

Its last king, Attalos III, willed the city to the Roman Empire so that its glory would not be spoiled by war. This proved to be a wise move because the Romans respected its cultural glory and religious character, making Pergamum the capital of the province of Asia Minor for a period of time. The Romans also left their mark on the city when it became the first city in which the cult of "divine" Caesars was established.

Pergamum

PLANNING NOTES:

Small Group Bible Discovery (10 minutes)

> *Participant's Guide pages 64–76.*
>
> During this time, a group with fewer than seven participants will stay together. A group larger than seven participants will break into small groups. Assign each group one of the following topics. If you have more than five small groups, assign some topics to more than one group.

Let's break into groups of three to five—people sitting near you—and study some Bible passages and truths mentioned in the video.

Turn to pages 64–76 in your Participant's Guide. There you'll find a list of five topics. You'll have ten minutes to read and discuss the topic I'll assign to you.

> Assign each group a topic.

I'll signal you when one minute is left.

Topic A: The Struggle Between God and Satan (Evil)

Since before the human race was created, a great battle has taken place between God and Satan. The early Christians realized that the gods of their pagan neighbors were, in fact, counterfeits of Satan designed to deceive them and lure them away from following God.

1. What basic conflict is described throughout the Bible? (See Genesis 3:1–15; Revelation 12:7–11.)

   Suggested Responses: the battle between Satan and his followers and God and His followers.

2. During His ministry on earth, what did Jesus demonstrate and accomplish related to the battle between God and Satan? (See Matthew 8:28–32; 12:22–28; Mark 1:21–27; Hebrews 2:14–15.)

   Suggested Responses: Jesus demonstrated His power over demons (which the demons recognized), and through His death on the cross Jesus destroyed Satan's power over physical death and made it possible for people to be set free from bondage to sin.

3. What role in this battle did Jesus assign to His disciples, and in what way(s) did He encourage them? (See Matthew 10:1, 7–8; Luke 10:17–20.)

   Suggested Responses: Jesus gave them authority to drive out evil spirits, heal every disease and sickness, and overcome all of Satan's power. He also told them of the impact they had on Satan and reminded them that their true source of joy was their spiritual status in heaven, not what they could accomplish.

4. What is Satan's nature, and what does he try to accomplish? (See Genesis 3:1–5; Matthew 4:1–4; John 8:44; 2 Corinthians 11:13–14.)

   Suggested Responses: Satan is a murderer and the "father of lies"; he "masquerades as an angel of light"; he tries to lead people away from God; he preys on

small Group Bible Discovery

Topic A: The Struggle Between God and Satan (Evil)

Since before the human race was created, a great battle has taken place between God and Satan. The early Christians realized that the gods of their pagan neighbors were, in fact, counterfeits of Satan designed to deceive them and lure them away from following God.

1. What basic conflict is described throughout the Bible? (See Genesis 3:1–15; Revelation 12:7–11.)

2. During His ministry on earth, what did Jesus demonstrate and accomplish related to the battle between God and Satan? (See Matthew 8:28–32; 12:22–28; Mark 1:21–27; Hebrews 2:14–15.)

3. What role in this battle did Jesus assign to His disciples, and in what way(s) did He encourage them? (See Matthew 10:1, 7–8; Luke 10:17–20.)

4. What is Satan's nature and what does he try to accomplish? (See Genesis 3:1–5; Matthew 4:1–4; John 8:44; 2 Corinthians 11:13–14.)

5. In contrast to what Satan wants people to think, who is really in charge of this world? (See Ephesians 1:18–23; 1 Timothy 6:13–16.)

THE TRUTH OF THE MATTER:

Giving God the Honor He Is Due

Satan has always wanted to rob God of the credit and honor due to Him. Because the deified emperors and gods of Pergamum such as Asclepius, Demeter, Dionysius, and Zeus received credit and honor that was due to God alone, they were demonic counterfeits. Things haven't changed much in our world today. Satan still wants people to believe that we have the authority to decide what's ours, what's right and wrong, and so on.

Our culture has bought into Satan's lie. People today (most Christians included) act as if credit is due the hard worker, the educated and successful people, people who care for their physical bodies properly, etc. But this perspective denies that God alone is Lord and provides everything we need—food, health, joy, wealth, etc. As the pagan cults of Pergamum illustrate, there is no place for God when we assume that perspective. *Anyone who fails to give God the credit He deserves is where Satan lives! Satan rules where people take credit for things due God, or give His honor to others.*

If Christians are to be faithful witnesses to the Lord of Lords and King of Kings, we must choose a different perspective. We must give Him credit and honor for *all* that He has provided and done for us. God is Lord of all and must be praised for all!

our physical weaknesses, as he tried to do when he tempted Jesus in the wilderness; etc.

✏ 5.   In contrast to what Satan wants people to think, who is really in charge of this world? (See Ephesians 1:18–23; 1 Timothy 6:13–16.)

Suggested Responses: God alone is ruler, the King of Kings and Lord of Lords; God has such power that He raised Jesus from the dead and seated Him in the heavenly realms; God has placed Jesus in authority over all things, including Satan; etc.

THE TRUTH OF THE MATTER

Giving God the Honor He Is Due

Satan has always wanted to rob God of the credit and honor due to Him. Because the deified emperors and gods of Pergamum such as Asclepius, Demeter, Dionysus, and Zeus received credit and honor that was due to God alone, they were demonic counterfeits. Things haven't changed much in our world today. Satan still wants people to believe that we have the authority to decide what's ours, what's right and wrong, and so on.

Our culture has bought into Satan's lie. People today (most Christians included) act as if credit is due the hard worker, the educated and successful people, people who care for their physical bodies properly, etc. But this perspective denies that God alone is Lord and provides everything we need— food, health, joy, wealth, etc. As the pagan cults of Pergamum illustrate, there is no place for God when we assume that perspective. *Anyone who fails to give God the credit He deserves is where Satan lives! Satan rules where people take credit for things due God, or give His honor to others.*

If Christians are to be faithful witnesses to the Lord of Lords and King of Kings, we must choose a different perspective. We must give Him credit and honor for *all* that He has provided and done for us. God is Lord of all and must be praised for all!

Topic B: Jesus Prepared His Disciples

Dionysus

Satan is diabolically clever and has deceived people from the beginning of human history. It is remarkable how closely the ancient pagan religions imitated and claimed to provide the same blessings that God provides. Knowing what His followers would encounter in pagan cities such as Pergamum, Jesus prepared them well to refute Satan's claims. Notice how He prepared them to deal with each of the claims below.

✏ 1.   The priests of Dionysus claimed that their god could turn water into wine, but it was done in his temple in secret. (See John 2:1–11.)

4. What is Satan's nature and what does he try to accomplish? (See Genesis 3:1–5; Matthew 4:1–4; John 8:44; 2 Corinthians 11:13–14.)

5. In contrast to what Satan wants people to think, who is really in charge of this world? (See Ephesians 1:18–23; 1 Timothy 6:13–16.)

THE TRUTH OF THE MATTER:

Giving God the Honor He Is Due

Satan has always wanted to rob God of the credit and honor due to Him. Because the deified emperors and gods of Pergamum such as Asclepius, Demeter, Dionysus, and Zeus received credit and honor that was due to God alone, they were demonic counterfeits. Things haven't changed much in our world today. Satan still wants people to believe that we have the authority to decide what's ours, what's right and wrong, and so on.

Our culture has bought into Satan's lie. People today (most Christians included) act as if credit is due the hard worker, the educated and successful people, people who care for their physical bodies properly, etc. But this perspective denies that God alone is Lord and provides everything we need—food, health, joy, wealth, etc. As the pagan cults of Pergamum illustrate, there is no place for God when we assume that perspective. *Anyone who fails to give God the credit He deserves is where Satan lives! Satan rules where people take credit for things due God, or give His honor to others.*

If Christians are to be faithful witnesses to the Lord of Lords and King of Kings, we must choose a different perspective. We must give Him credit and honor for *all* that He has provided and done for us. God is Lord of all and must be praised for all!

Topic B: Jesus Prepared His Disciples

Satan is diabolically clever and has deceived people from the beginning of human history. It is remarkable how closely the ancient pagan religions imitated and claimed to provide the same blessings that God provides. Knowing what His followers would encounter in pagan cities such as Pergamum, Jesus prepared them well to refute Satan's claims. Notice how He prepared them to deal with each of the claims below.

Dionysus

1. The priests of Dionysus claimed that their god could turn water into wine, but it was done in his temple in secret. (See John 2:1–11.)

2. Demeter, the goddess of grain, supposedly provided daily food for people. (See Matthew 4:4; 14:19; John 6:1–14.)

3. The followers of Demeter believed that she offered them the possibility of resurrection and forgiveness of sins through ceremonial washing in bulls' blood. (See John 11:17–26, 38–44; 20:26–30; 1 Corinthians 15:3–8; Hebrews 9:11–14.)

Suggested Response: In His first miracle, Jesus turned water into wine in broad daylight in front of witnesses.

2. Demeter, the goddess of grain, supposedly provided daily food for people. (See Matthew 4:4; 14:19; John 6:1–14.)

Suggested Responses: Jesus clearly viewed daily provision as coming from God; He thanked God for the five loaves and two fish before He multiplied them; etc.

3. The followers of Demeter believed that she offered them the possibility of resurrection and forgiveness of sins through ceremonial washing in bulls' blood. (See John 11:17–26, 38–44; 20:26–30; 1 Corinthians 15:3–8; Hebrews 9:11–14.)

Asclepius

Suggested Responses: Jesus stated that He was the resurrection and the life and that those who believe in Him will never die; He demonstrated His power over death by raising Lazarus from the dead; He rose from the dead Himself and was seen by a number of people; through His shed blood—not the blood of any animal—people can receive forgiveness for their sins; etc.

4. Asclepius was known as the god of healing and received honor from those who had been healed. (See John 5:1–13.)

Suggested Responses: Jesus—the only true healer—healed an invalid man simply by speaking to him. The invalid had waited for thirty-eight years by the Pool of Bethesda because he believed the pool had healing properties. Jesus did not heal the man to gain glory for Himself. In fact, the man didn't even know who healed him!

Asclepius

Note: Apparently there was a small Asclepius temple near the Pool of Bethesda, so it is possible that the myth of Asclepius's healing powers using moving water had been transferred to the pool. Certainly people were cured in the Asclepius hospital—by psychological suggestion, demonic powers, or effective medical knowledge of the day. What's important is that Asclepius had to be given full credit and honor for any healing that occurred.

5. Zeus, whose temple could be seen from a great distance, claimed to be the giver of life, lord of all, and creator of all. (See John 1:1–3; 10:10; 11:25–26, 41–44; Revelation 17:14.)

Suggested Responses: Jesus raised people from the dead, giving them life; all things were made through Him, and nothing was made without Him; He taught

Topic B: Jesus Prepared His Disciples

Satan is diabolically clever and has deceived people from the beginning of human history. It is remarkable how closely the ancient pagan religions imitated and claimed to provide the same blessings that God provides. Knowing what His followers would encounter in pagan cities such as Pergamum, Jesus prepared them well to refute Satan's claims. Notice how He prepared them to deal with each of the claims below.

Dionysus

1. The priests of Dionysus claimed that their god could turn water into wine, but it was done in his temple in secret. (See John 2:1–11.)

2. Demeter, the goddess of grain, supposedly provided daily food for people. (See Matthew 4:4; 14:19; John 6:1–14.)

3. The followers of Demeter believed that she offered them the possibility of resurrection and forgiveness of sins through ceremonial washing in bulls' blood. (See John 11:17–26, 38–44; 20:26–30; 1 Corinthians 15:3–8; Hebrews 9:11–14.)

Asclepius   **Asclepius**

4. Asclepius was known as the god of healing and received honor from those who had been healed. (See John 5:1–13.)

5. Zeus, whose temple could be seen from a great distance, claimed to be the giver of life, lord of all, and creator of all. (See John 1:1–3; 10:10; 11:25–26, 41–44; Revelation 17:14.)

6. The Roman emperor, who declared himself to be the son of a god, lord of all, and the source of truth, demanded to be worshiped as god. (See John 1:10–11; 12:27–33; Acts 1:4–11.)

PLANNING NOTES:

that He had come to give people abundant life; He is called Lord of Lords and King of Kings; etc.

✏ 6. The Roman emperor, who declared himself to be the son of a god, lord of all, and the source of truth, demanded to be worshiped as god. (See John 1:10–11; 12:27–33; Acts 1:4–11.)

Suggested Responses: Jesus was declared to be the Son of the God of heaven; people heard a voice thunder from heaven glorifying the name of God; Jesus ascended to heaven while His disciples watched; etc.

DATA FILE

Clever Counterfeits: The False Claims of the Cults

Each of the cults in Pergamum was a counterfeit, a clever copy of things that God alone provides. Each god took credit or honor away from God, thus giving it to something human or of human invention.

False Gods	False Claim(s)	The Truth
Zeus	Acclaimed as king of kings, lord of lords, creator of the universe.	God alone is King of Kings, Lord of Lords, Creator of the universe.
Dionysus	Reputed to provide joy, eternal life, and meaning; said to be able to change water into wine.	God alone provides these through Jesus, who turned water into wine and rose from the dead.
Demeter	Said to provide daily bread, resurrection, and eternal life through the blood of animals.	God alone provides these through Jesus, who fed thousands of people miraculously and shed His blood and rose from the dead so that people might receive eternal life.
Asclepius	Reputed to provide good health, healing from disease, and eternal life.	God alone provides these through Jesus, who healed many people, rose from the dead, and provides eternal life.
Emperor Worship	Emperor was viewed as lord of all, the supreme source of truth in the universe.	Jesus, seated at God's right hand, is Lord of Lords and King of the universe; God is the source of all truth.
People Today	Give themselves or other things credit for what God has really done (healing, etc.).	People today need to have a personal relationship with the one, true God through Jesus the Messiah.

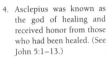
Asclepius

Asclepius

4. Asclepius was known as the god of healing and received honor from those who had been healed. (See John 5:1–13.)

5. Zeus, whose temple could be seen from a great distance, claimed to be the giver of life, lord of all, and creator of all. (See John 1:1–3; 10:10; 11:25–26, 41–44; Revelation 17:14.)

6. The Roman emperor, who declared himself to be the son of a god, lord of all, and the source of truth, demanded to be worshiped as god. (See John 1:10–11; 12:27–33; Acts 1:4–11.)

---

68   Faith Lessons on the Early Church

DATA FILE

Clever Counterfeits: The False Claims of the Cults

Each of the cults in Pergamum was a counterfeit, a clever copy of things that God alone provides. Each god took credit or honor away from God, thus giving it to something human or of human invention.

False Gods	False Claim(s)	The Truth
Zeus	Acclaimed as king of kings, lord of lords, creator of the universe.	God alone is King of Kings, Lord of Lords, Creator of the universe.
Dionysus	Reputed to provide joy, eternal life, and meaning; said to be able to change water into wine.	God alone provides these through Jesus, who turned water into wine and rose from the dead.
Demeter	Said to provide daily bread, resurrection, and eternal life through the blood of animals.	God alone provides these through Jesus, who fed thousands of people miraculously and shed His blood and rose from the dead so that people might receive eternal life.
Asclepius	Reputed to provide good health, healing from disease, and eternal life.	God alone provides these through Jesus, who healed many people, rose from the dead, and provides eternal life.
Emperor Worship	Emperor was viewed as lord of all, the supreme source of truth in the universe.	Jesus, seated at God's right hand, is Lord of Lords and King of the universe; God is the source of all truth.
People Today	Give themselves or other things credit for what God has really done (healing, etc.).	People today need to have a personal relationship with the one, true God through Jesus the Messiah.

PLANNING NOTES:

Topic C: Standing Stones

As Christians, our ability to face the future is directly related to our awareness of how God has already worked in our lives. God's work in the past, whether the distant past or our own past, is the foundation on which our beliefs and commitment are built. Thus it is appropriate for God's people to establish "standing stones" as memorials to what God has done. Just as people in the cult of Asclepius inscribed their names and the ailment from which they were healed on standing stones to honor their false god, John described a "white stone with a new name written on it" (Revelation 2:17).

1. For each of the following passages, summarize the story or event mentioned and note the work of God that the standing stone commemorates or represents:

Scripture	Significance of the "Standing Stone"
Genesis 28:10–18	*Jacob set up a standing stone as a monument to God's presence in that place, which he recognized as a result of the dream God had given him.*
Joshua 4:1–9	*The Israelites took twelve stones—one for each tribe—from the middle of the Jordan River and set them up as a memorial to God's miraculous aid in crossing the Jordan River.*
Joshua 24:19–27	*Joshua set up a large stone to stand as a witness to the promises the Israelites had made to serve and obey God alone.*
Revelation 2:12–17	*God promised to honor each of His faithful followers in Pergamum with a white stone with a new name written on it.*

2. To what does Peter compare believers in 1 Peter 2:4–5?

   Suggested Responses: "living stones" that are being built into a house or building in which the presence of God lives; each believer is a living stone in the spiritual "house" of God.

3. What kind of lives are believers called to live—and why? How does this relate to the purpose of "standing stones"?

   Suggested Responses: Believers are to live godly lives so that the world will know that the Lord is God, so unbelievers will notice what we do and glorify God. In effect, our lives are to be "standing stones" that honor God's work in our lives and continually testify to His power and glory.

Topic C: Standing Stones

As Christians, our ability to face the future is directly related to our awareness of how God has already worked in our lives. God's work in the past, whether the distant past or our own past, is the foundation on which our beliefs and commitment are built. Thus it is appropriate for God's people to establish "standing stones" as memorials to what God has done. Just as people in the cult of Asclepius inscribed their names and the ailment from which they were healed on standing stones to honor their false god, John described a "white stone with a new name written on it" (Revelation 2:17).

1. For each of the following passages, summarize the story or event mentioned and note the work of God that the standing stone commemorates or represents:

Scripture	Significance of the "Standing Stone"
Genesis 28:10–18	
Joshua 4:1–9	
Joshua 24:19–27	
Revelation 2:12–17	

2. To what does Peter compare believers in 1 Peter 2:4–5?

3. What kind of lives are believers called to live—and why? How does this relate to the purpose of "standing stones"?

Topic D: Living in the Place Where Satan Lives

Satan's foremost purpose is to pull people away from God. He accomplishes this by making the pursuit of sin not only acceptable but also appealing, and by robbing God of the credit He alone deserves. Satan can be described as living or having his throne wherever such activities take place.

1. Note the pursuit of evil described elsewhere in Scripture that was also practiced in Pergamum.

   a. 2 Peter 2:9–14, 18–19

   b. 1 Corinthians 10:19–21

   c. 1 Corinthians 6:9

   d. 1 John 3:8

   e. Leviticus 17:10–12; Acts 15:19–20, 29

PLANNING NOTES:

Topic D: Living in the Place Where Satan Lives

Satan's foremost purpose is to pull people away from God. He accomplishes this by making the pursuit of sin not only acceptable but also appealing, and by robbing God of the credit He alone deserves. Satan can be described as living or having his throne wherever such activities take place.

1. Note the pursuit of evil described elsewhere in Scripture that was also practiced in Pergamum.

   a. 2 Peter 2:9–14, 18–19

   Suggested Responses: The unrighteous follow the corrupt desires of their sinful nature and despise authority. They carouse, commit sexual immorality, revel in physical pleasures, and sin continually. They promise freedom while they are slaves of depravity—appealing to the lustful desires of sinful human nature and seducing others to participate in evil. This description certainly fit the Dionysus cult.

   b. 1 Corinthians 10:19–21

   Suggested Responses: Paul says that the sacrifices of pagans are offered to demons, which clearly takes credit away from God and gives it to Satan. He goes on to say that you can't honor both God and Satan. The people of Pergamum sacrificed to Dionysus, Zeus, Asclepius, Demeter, as well as to other gods.

   c. 1 Corinthians 6:9

   Suggested Responses: People in Pergamum practiced idolatry, immorality, and drunkenness—all of which were evidence that they were not following God and, therefore, were following Satan.

   d. 1 John 3:8

   Suggested Responses: Anyone who does what is sinful is of the devil, so an entire community like Pergamum that practiced perversions was clearly under Satan's rule.

   e. Leviticus 17:10–12; Acts 15:19–20, 29

   Suggested Responses: The people of Pergamum, such as those in the Dionysus cult, ate raw meat with blood in it, which was a clear violation of God's law.

2. What is the responsibility of believers who live among evil people? (See 1 Peter 3:15–17.)

   Suggested Responses: to view Jesus as Lord, to always be ready to explain to people the source of the hope that God provides, to keep a clear conscience, to be willing to suffer for doing good, etc.

2. To what does Peter compare believers in 1 Peter 2:4–5?

3. What kind of lives are believers called to live—and why? How does this relate to the purpose of "standing stones"?

Topic D: Living in the Place Where Satan Lives

Satan's foremost purpose is to pull people away from God. He accomplishes this by making the pursuit of sin not only acceptable but also appealing, and by robbing God of the credit He alone deserves. Satan can be described as living or having his throne wherever such activities take place.

1. Note the pursuit of evil described elsewhere in Scripture that was also practiced in Pergamum.

   a. 2 Peter 2:9–14, 18–19

   b. 1 Corinthians 10:19–21

   c. 1 Corinthians 6:9

   d. 1 John 3:8

   e. Leviticus 17:10–12; Acts 15:19–20, 29

2. What is the responsibility of believers who live among evil people? (See 1 Peter 3:15–17.)

DATA FILE

Five Candidates for "Satan's Throne"

Altar of Zeus

There are many opinions as to exactly what John referred to when he wrote these phrases in Revelation 2:13: "where Satan has his throne" and "where Satan lives." No one knows whether he had in mind a specific temple or pagan practice, or whether the sum of the evil activities in Pergamum made the city the home of Satan. In a sense, all of the following pagan centers could be identified as strongholds of Satan.

The Great Altar of Zeus

Around 250 B.C., the people of Pergamum won a great victory against the Galatians. In memory of that event, they built a great altar to Zeus, who was considered to be king of the gods, the life-giver, the lord of all, the creator of all—titles that belong to God alone. Located on the west side of the Acropolis more than one thousand feet above the valley, the altar of Zeus smoked day and night with sacrifices. It could be seen from a great distance and was shaped like an ancient throne. Built on a podium 105 feet by 110 feet, the forty-foot-high altar was the largest in the world. It had three tiers with steps on one side, and each tier had a carved marble frieze featuring scenes of Zeus mythology, which was extremely immoral. Today, the entire altar is in the Pergamum Museum in Berlin.

(continued on page 72)

DATA FILE

Five Candidates for "Satan's Throne"

There are many opinions as to exactly what John referred to when he wrote these phrases in Revelation 2:13: "where Satan has his throne" and "where Satan lives." No one knows whether he had in mind a specific temple or pagan practice, or whether the sum of the evil activities in Pergamum made the city the home of Satan. In a sense, all of the following pagan centers could be identified as strongholds of Satan.

The Great Altar of Zeus

Altar of Zeus

Around 250 B.C., the people of Pergamum won a great victory against the Galatians. In memory of that event, they built a great altar to Zeus, who was considered to be king of the gods, the life-giver, the lord of all, the creator of all—titles that belong to God alone. Located on the west side of the Acropolis more than one thousand feet above the valley, the altar of Zeus smoked day and night with sacrifices. It could be seen from a great distance and was shaped like an ancient throne. Built on a podium 105 feet by 110 feet, the forty-foot-high altar was the largest in the world. It had three tiers with steps on one side, and each tier had a carved marble frieze featuring scenes of Zeus mythology, which was extremely immoral. Today, the entire altar is in the Pergamum Museum in Berlin.

Dionysus Temple and Cult Center

Dionysus Temple

Originally built in the third century before Christ, this small, beautiful temple was remodeled by the Romans. It was approached by a twenty-five-step stairway at the end of a 770-foot terrace. Here, people worshiped Dionysus, the fertility god of the vine who was also known as the god of ecstasy, particularly because of the wine he supposedly provided and the orgies related to his worship. During festivals that celebrated him, worshipers consumed wine in great abundance and gorged on raw meat from Dionysus's sacred animal—the bull—all in an effort to be mystically joined to him.

The cult center is believed to have been located on the south side of the Acropolis, near wine shops and a bath house. This center is eighty feet long and thirty-two feet wide. A niche for the idol of Dionysus was positioned to the right of a marble altar. Murals depicting the Dionysus practices were found in frescoes on the low walls around the room. The wine shop next door had several large, baked-clay jars buried in the floor that probably contained wine used in various cultic practices or sold to the public.

Dionysus was considered to be the source of fertility for the grapevines, and one of his symbols was the phallus. He was also viewed as the source of life, so ceremonies dedicated to him included a variety of sexually immoral practices. The cult attracted the common people because it promised eternal life to worshipers and catered to human lusts aroused by the pagan cults. Drunkenness and sexual immorality was so extreme during celebrations in Dionysus's honor that his worship was banned for a time in Rome because it was too perverted! Again, Satan created a counterfeit to take credit for things of God: eternal life, happiness, purpose, and fertility.

(continued on page 114)

2. What is the responsibility of believers who live among evil people? (See 1 Peter 3:15–17.)

DATA FILE

Five Candidates for "Satan's Throne"

Altar of Zeus

There are many opinions as to exactly what John referred to when he wrote these phrases in Revelation 2:13: "where Satan has his throne" and "where Satan lives." No one knows whether he had in mind a specific temple or pagan practice, or whether the sum of the evil activities in Pergamum made the city the home of Satan. In a sense, all of the following pagan centers could be identified as strongholds of Satan.

The Great Altar of Zeus

Around 250 B.C., the people of Pergamum won a great victory against the Galatians. In memory of that event, they built a great altar to Zeus, who was considered to be king of the gods, the life-giver, the lord of all, the creator of all—titles that belong to God alone. Located on the west side of the Acropolis more than one thousand feet above the valley, the altar of Zeus smoked day and night with sacrifices. It could be seen from a great distance and was shaped like an ancient throne. Built on a podium 105 feet by 110 feet, the forty-foot-high altar was the largest in the world. It had three tiers with steps on one side, and each tier had a carved marble frieze featuring scenes of Zeus mythology, which was extremely immoral. Today, the entire altar is in the Pergamum Museum in Berlin.

(continued on page 72)

(continued from page 71)

Dionysus Temple and Cult Center

Dionysus Temple

Originally built in the third century before Christ, this small, beautiful temple was remodeled by the Romans. It was approached by a twenty-five-step stairway at the end of a 770-foot terrace. Here, people worshiped Dionysus, the fertility god of the vine who was also known as the god of ecstasy, particularly because of the wine he supposedly provided and the orgies related to his worship. During festivals that celebrated him, worshipers consumed wine in great abundance and gorged on raw meat from Dionysus's sacred animal—the bull—all in an effort to be mystically joined to him.

The cult center is believed to have been located on the south side of the Acropolis, near wine shops and a bath house. This center is eighty feet long and thirty-two feet wide. A niche for the idol of Dionysus was positioned to the right of a marble altar. Murals depicting the Dionysus practices were found in frescoes on the low walls around the room. The wine shop next door had several large, baked-clay jars buried in the floor that probably contained wine used in various cultic practices or sold to the public.

Dionysus was considered to be the source of fertility for the grapevines, and one of his symbols was the phallus. He was also viewed as the source of life, so ceremonies dedicated to him included a variety of sexually immoral practices. The cult attracted the common people because it promised eternal life to worshipers and catered to human lusts aroused by the pagan cults. Drunkenness and sexual immorality was so extreme during celebrations in Dionysus's honor that his worship was banned for a time in Rome because it was too perverted! Again, Satan created a counterfeit to take credit for things of God: eternal life, happiness, purpose, and fertility.

(continued from page 112)

Demeter: The Goddess of Groceries

Believed to be the goddess of grain who provided food, Demeter was popular among common people because acquiring enough food was a dominant concern for them. This secretive cult worshiped in a temple (twenty-two by forty feet) and eight-hundred-seat theater complex on the south side of the acropolis of Pergamum. It was also known for its death-resurrection theme that focused on Demeter's daughter who was allowed to spend half the year in Hades and the other half on earth. Thus adherents believed that Demeter offered them the possibility of resurrection.

Although little is known about the rituals of this religion, there was an initiation ceremony involving the blood of a bull. The initiate would stand or lie at the bottom of a pit while a bull was slaughtered above on a grid. The blood would wash over the new convert, providing redemptive cleansing—a clever imitation of salvation through Jesus' shed blood on the cross.

The Cult of Asclepius

The Pool in Asclepion

Asclepius, the god who healed with moving water, was said to be the son of the god Apollo and a woman named Coronis. His symbol was the snake, and he was known as the god of life because the snake seemingly resurrects itself (sheds its skin and is born anew, disappears to hibernate and reappears each year). Live snakes were kept in a sacred chest in each of his temples.

Asclepius was also known as "Asclepius Savior." Hospitals or treatment centers were frequently located in conjunction with his temples, and people flocked to Pergamum from all over the world to seek healing at the large Asclepion there. The healing process was a mixture of religious ceremony and health practices—especially diet, water, herbs, and exercise.

When patients entered the Asclepion (hospital) in Pergamum after traveling the kilometer-long "sacred way," they were greeted at the gate by temple priests who would interview them to determine their acceptability for healing. Old people and pregnant women nearing the time of delivery were excluded (no deaths or births were allowed within the sanctuary), as were those who were considered impure. This is an interesting parallel to modern-day cultures that seek to terminate the lives of senior citizens and the unborn.

Each patient who was admitted made an offering (probably incense) to show his or her devotion to Asclepius and began receiving free, supervised treatment. As part of the healing process, "sacred water" from a spring and a well was used for bathing and drinking. Treatments included mud baths, special diet, exercise, stress relief, and exposure to the sun. (Perhaps some of the patients' sleep was drug induced.)

Any healing that took place—whether as the result of psychological suggestion, demonic powers, and/or the medical knowledge of the day—was credited to Asclepius. Healed people would bow to the statue of Asclepius and the sacred snake to offer thanks, make an offering—apparently a pig—and have their names and the ailments Asclepius had cured inscribed on a marble pillar (usually white). Finally, each healed person would leave a gift with the priests to thank the god and would witness to many other people about Asclepius's great ability to heal. Thus many people heard or saw the praise and honor given to Asclepius, which in turn increased the cult's popularity.

Emperor Worship

The center of Roman administration of the province of Asia, Pergamum was also the source and center of emperor worship in the Roman Empire. Julius Caesar was honored with a statue as early as 63 B.C. Emperor Augustus was

(continued on page 116)

Demeter: The Goddess of Groceries

Believed to be the goddess of grain who provided food, Demeter was popular among common people because acquiring enough food was a dominant concern for them. This secretive cult worshiped in a temple (twenty-two by forty feet) and eight-hundred-seat theater complex on the south side of the acropolis of Pergamum. It was also known for its death-resurrection theme that focused on Demeter's daughter who was allowed to spend half the year in Hades and the other half on earth. Thus adherents believed that Demeter offered them the possibility of resurrection.

Although little is known about the rituals of this religion, there was an initiation ceremony involving the blood of a bull. The initiate would stand or lie at the bottom of a pit while a bull was slaughtered above on a grid. The blood would wash over the new convert, providing redemptive cleansing—a clever imitation of salvation through Jesus' shed blood on the cross.

The Cult of Asclepius

The Pool in Asclepion

Asclepius, the god who healed with moving water, was said to be the son of the god Apollo and a woman named Coronis. His symbol was the snake and he was known as the god of life because the snake seemingly resurrects itself (sheds its skin and is born anew, disappears to hibernate and reappears each year). Live snakes were kept in a sacred chest in each of his temples.

Asclepius was also known as "Asclepius Savior." Hospitals or treatment centers were frequently located in conjunction with his temples, and people flocked to Pergamum from all over the world to seek healing at the large Asclepion there. The healing process was a mixture of religious ceremony and health practices—especially diet, water, herbs, and exercise.

When patients entered the Asclepion (hospital) in Pergamum after traveling the kilometer-long "sacred way," they were greeted at the gate

(continued on page 74)

(continued from page 73)

by temple priests who would interview them to determine their acceptability for healing. Old people and pregnant women nearing the time of delivery were excluded (no deaths or births were allowed within the sanctuary), as were those who were considered impure. This is an interesting parallel to modern-day cultures that seek to terminate the lives of senior citizens and the unborn.

Each patient who was admitted made an offering (probably incense) to show his or her devotion to Asclepius and began receiving free, supervised treatment. As part of the healing process, "sacred water" from a spring and a well was used for bathing and drinking. Treatments included mud baths, special diet, exercise, stress relief, and exposure to the sun. (Perhaps some of the patients' sleep was drug induced.)

Any healing that took place—whether as the result of psychological suggestion, demonic powers, and/or the medical knowledge of the day—was credited to Asclepius. Healed people would bow to the statue of Asclepius and the sacred snake to offer thanks, make an offering—apparently a pig—and have their names and the ailments Asclepius had cured inscribed on a marble pillar (usually white). Finally, each healed person would leave a gift with the priests to thank the god and would witness to many other people about Asclepius's great ability to heal. Thus many people heard or saw the praise and honor given to Asclepius, which in turn increased the cult's popularity.

Emperor Worship

The center of Roman administration of the province of Asia, Pergamum was also the source and center of emperor worship in the Roman Empire. Julius Caesar was honored with a statue as early as 63 B.C. Emperor Augustus was worshiped in the precinct of Athena, and a bronze statue of the emperor (now in the Vatican Museum) was placed there in 31 B.C., making Pergamum the first city in the empire to have an emperor cult.

On Caesar Augustus's birthday, the people of Pergamum worshiped him with processions, sacrifices, and a choir singing hymns in his honor. Once a year, everyone in the province was commanded to put incense on

(continued from page 114)

worshiped in the precinct of Athena, and a bronze statue of the emperor (now in the Vatican Museum) was placed there in 31 B.C., making Pergamum the first city in the empire to have an emperor cult.

On Caesar Augustus's birthday, the people of Pergamum worshiped him with processions, sacrifices, and a choir singing hymns in his honor. Once a year, everyone in the province was commanded to put incense on the altar of "divine" Caesar and declare, "Caesar is lord." This soon led to significant persecution of Christians, who would not make such a declaration because "Jesus is Lord." They refused to give the emperor honor due to God alone. Possibly the martyr Antipas mentioned in Revelation 2:13 was killed for refusing to worship the emperor. He is the only person besides Jesus who is called a "faithful" or "true" witness in the Bible.

Topic E: But It's Just Food!

1. What was the one complaint God had against the Christians in Pergamum? (See Revelation 2:14–16.)

    Suggested Response: Some of them held to the teachings of Balaam and the Nicolaitans and ate food sacrificed to idols.

2. Why was the eating of food sacrificed to idols of such significance?

    a. In the Old Testament? (See Numbers 25:1–3.)

    Suggested Responses: because eating sacrifices to gods, sexual immorality, and the worship of false gods went hand in hand to lead Israel away from God.

    b. In the New Testament? (See 1 Corinthians 8:4–13; 10:18–21.)

    Suggested Responses: Even though food sacrificed to idols is meaningless because the idols are fake gods, eating it still represents participation with evil, and Christians who have a relationship with God cannot pursue a relationship with evil (in this case, demons); eating food sacrificed to idols could also cause another Christian to sin, which would make the practice unthinkable.

3. What was so offensive about eating raw meat, meat with blood in it?

    a. In the Old Testament? (See Leviticus 17:10–14.)

    Suggested Responses: God prohibited the Israelites from eating meat with blood in it because the life of the creature is in the blood.

    b. In the New Testament? (See Acts 15:19–20, 29.)

    Suggested Responses: This was probably done out of respect for the life that the animal had given.

4. Identify and discuss our cultural equivalents to eating food sacrificed to idols and eating meat with blood in it—activities that are so strongly associated with a pagan worldview that they must be avoided.

    Suggested Responses: will vary. Encourage participants to carefully examine even the activities that we accept as a "normal" part of life and determine if those activities convey a spiritual message.

the altar of "divine" Caesar and declare, "Caesar is lord." This soon led to significant persecution of Christians, who would not make such a declaration because "Jesus is Lord." They refused to give the emperor honor due to God alone. Possibly the martyr Antipas mentioned in Revelation 2:13 was killed for refusing to worship the emperor. He is the only person besides Jesus who is called a "faithful" or "true" witness in the Bible.

Topic E: But It's Just Food!

1. What was the complaint God had against the Christians in Pergamum? (See Revelation 2:14–16.)

2. Why was the eating of food sacrificed to idols of such significance?

   a. In the Old Testament? (See Numbers 25:1–3.)

   b. In the New Testament? (See 1 Corinthians 8:4–13; 10:18–21.)

3. What was so offensive about eating raw meat, meat with blood in it?

   a. In the Old Testament? (See Leviticus 17:10–14.)

   b. In the New Testament? (See Acts 15:19–20, 29.)

4. Identify and discuss our cultural equivalents to eating food sacrificed to idols and eating meat with blood in it—activities that are so strongly associated with a pagan worldview that they must be avoided.

DID YOU KNOW?

In Revelation 2:15, the apostle John condemns those who follow the teachings of Balaam and the Nicolaitans. Balaam is known for his role in encouraging the Israelites to participate in the feasts and sexual immorality of the Canaanite idols, which led them away from God. Scholars disagree about who the Nicolaitans were. According to church tradition, they comprised a group of people who believed that since they were redeemed by Jesus and, therefore, free in Him, they could participate in immoral ceremonies since idols were not gods anyway. Interestingly, both words mean the same thing, "prince of the people." Biblical writers strongly condemned participation in such behavior (1 Corinthians 10:20–22) for many reasons, including the fact that Christians were not to eat meat or drink wine that had been used in sacrifices to pagan gods.

PLANNING NOTES:

DID YOU KNOW?

In Revelation 2:15, the apostle John condemns those who follow the teachings of Balaam and the Nicolaitans. Balaam is known for his role in encouraging the Israelites to participate in the feasts and sexual immorality of the Canaanite idols, which led them away from God. Scholars disagree about who the Nicolaitans were. According to church tradition, they comprised a group of people who believed that since they were redeemed by Jesus and, therefore, free in Him, they could participate in immoral ceremonies since idols were not gods anyway. Interestingly, both words mean the same thing, "prince of the people." Biblical writers strongly condemned participation in such behavior (1 Corinthians 10:20–22) for many reasons, including the fact that Christians were not to eat meat or drink wine that had been used in sacrifices to pagan gods.

Signal the groups when one minute remains so that they may wrap up their discovery time.

faith Lesson

9 minutes

Time for Reflection (4 minutes)

It's time for each of us to think quietly about how we can do a better job of standing for God in an evil world. On page 77 of the Participant's Guide, you'll find a passage of Scripture. Let's each read this passage silently and take the next few minutes to consider some of the questions that follow.

Please do not talk during this time. It's a time when we all can reflect on today's lesson and how it applies to our lives.

The Scripture passage and questions are reproduced in their entirety in the Participant's Guide on page 77.

The acts of the sinful nature are obvious: sexual immorality, impurity and debauchery; idolatry and witchcraft; hatred, discord, jealousy, fits of rage, selfish ambition, dissensions, factions and envy; drunkenness, orgies, and the like. I warn you, as I did before, that those who live like this will not inherit the kingdom of God.

But the fruit of the Spirit is love, joy, peace, patience, kindness, goodness, faithfulness, gentleness and self-control. Against such things there is no law. Those who belong to Christ Jesus have crucified the sinful nature with its passions and desires. Since we live by the Spirit, let us keep in step with the Spirit. (Galatians 5:19–25)

It's easy to make excuses for sinful behavior that is accepted as "normal" in society. In what ways do you make excuses to indulge in your sinful nature rather than to keep in step with the Spirit?

3. What was so offensive about eating raw meat, meat with blood in it?

   a. In the Old Testament? (See Leviticus 17:10–14.)

   b. In the New Testament? (See Acts 15:19–20, 29.)

4. Identify and discuss our cultural equivalents to eating food sacrificed to idols and eating meat with blood in it—activities that are so strongly associated with a pagan worldview that they must be avoided.

DID YOU KNOW?

In Revelation 2:15, the apostle John condemns those who follow the teachings of Balaam and the Nicolaitans. Balaam is known for his role in encouraging the Israelites to participate in the feasts and sexual immorality of the Canaanite idols, which led them away from God. Scholars disagree about who the Nicolaitans were. According to church tradition, they comprised a group of people who believed that since they were redeemed by Jesus and, therefore, free in Him, they could participate in immoral ceremonies since idols were not gods anyway. Interestingly, both words mean the same thing, "prince of the people." Biblical writers strongly condemned participation in such behavior (1 Corinthians 10:20–22) for many reasons, including the fact that Christians were not to eat meat or drink wine that had been used in sacrifices to pagan gods.

faith Lesson

Time for Reflection

Read the following Scripture passage and take the next few minutes to consider how you can do a better job of standing for God in an evil world.

> The acts of the sinful nature are obvious: sexual immorality, impurity and debauchery; idolatry and witchcraft; hatred, discord, jealousy, fits of rage, selfish ambition, dissensions, factions and envy; drunkenness, orgies, and the like. I warn you, as I did before, that those who live like this will not inherit the kingdom of God.
>
> But the fruit of the Spirit is love, joy, peace, patience, kindness, goodness, faithfulness, gentleness and self-control. Against such things there is no law. Those who belong to Christ Jesus have crucified the sinful nature with its passions and desires. Since we live by the Spirit, let us keep in step with the Spirit.
>
> GALATIANS 5:19–25

It's easy to make excuses for sinful behavior that is accepted as "normal" in society. In what ways do you make excuses to indulge in your sinful nature rather than to keep in step with the Spirit?

Consider for a moment the difference in testimony between a Christian who gives into temptations versus one who lives by the Spirit. What kind of an impact would each one have on a watching world?

In what specific areas do you need to reaffirm your submission to Christ's lordship and live more in accordance with His Spirit?

Action Points

Take a moment to jot down an action step (or steps) that you will commit to this week as a result of what you have learned.

1. *The host of pagan gods worshiped in Pergamum encouraged people to seek what they needed for life somewhere other*

Consider for a moment the difference in testimony between a Christian who gives into temptations versus one who lives by the Spirit. What kind of an impact would each one have on a watching world?

In what specific areas do you need to reaffirm your submission to Christ's lordship and live more in accordance with His Spirit?

Action Points (5 minutes)

> The following points are reproduced on pages 77–80 of the Participant's Guide.

Now it's time to wrap up our session.

> Give participants a moment to transition from their thoughtfulness to giving you their full attention.

I'd like to take a moment to summarize the key points we explored. After I have reviewed these points, I will give you a moment to jot down an action step (or steps) that you will commit to this week as a result of what you have learned today.

> Read the following points and pause afterward so that participants can consider and write out their commitment.

1. *The host of pagan gods worshiped in Pergamum encouraged people to seek what they needed for life somewhere other than from God. Perhaps that's why John wrote that Satan "lived" in that city, which was noted for its many shrines and temples.*

   People were drawn to the wine drinking and sexual license as well as the promise of physical healing, provision of food, forgiveness of sins, and immortality. Clearly Satan wanted people to believe that meaning and significance—even eternal life—could be found through themselves, false gods, or the world around them. Satan still offers this temptation to people today.

   In what way(s)—even the most subtle—are you tempted to try to find "life" through ways other than God?

   Identify the "gods" of this world that appeal most to you. What will you do to strengthen your spiritual "armor" against those specific temptations?

2. *Having been carefully prepared ahead of time by Jesus, John and the other early missionaries knew the truth about Satan's counterfeit blessings.* They knew that God and God alone is the source of all true blessings. John had witnessed Jesus' life and miracles firsthand and was prepared to refute the claims of false religions.

   Evaluate your personal preparedness to refute Satan's false claims:

than from God. Perhaps that's why John wrote that Satan "lived" in that city, which was noted for its many shrines and temples.

People were drawn to the wine drinking and sexual license as well as the promise of physical healing, provision of food, forgiveness of sins, and immortality. Clearly Satan wanted people to believe that meaning and significance—even eternal life—could be found through themselves, false gods, or the world around them. Satan still offers this temptation to people today.

In what way(s)—even the most subtle—are you tempted to try to find "life" through ways other than God?

Identify the "gods" of this world that appeal most to you. What will you do to strengthen your spiritual "armor" against those specific temptations?

2. *Having been carefully prepared ahead of time by Jesus, John and the other early missionaries knew the truth about Satan's counterfeit blessings.* They knew that God and God alone is the source of all true blessings. John had witnessed Jesus' life and miracles firsthand and was prepared to refute the claims of false religions.

Evaluate your personal preparedness to refute Satan's false claims:

Which of your personal experiences testify to God being the source of all truth and all blessings?

Which false teachings are you equipped to refute by using the Word of God?

3. *Using the imagery of the white stones inscribed by people who supposedly had been healed by Asclepius, John challenged believers in Pergamum to stand courageously as witnesses for God, telling what He had done in their lives and giving Him the credit He was due.*

Believers today have the important responsibility of expressing God's truth to a spiritually hungry world. We need to let people know what God has done for us and praise God for all that He has done—the "ordinary" as well as the extraordinary.

PLANNING NOTES:

Which of your personal experiences testify to God being the source of all truth and all blessings?

Which false teachings are you equipped to refute by using the Word of God?

3. *Using the imagery of the white stones inscribed by people who supposedly had been healed by Asclepius, John challenged believers in Pergamum to stand courageously as witnesses for God, telling what He had done in their lives and giving Him the credit He was due.*

Believers today have the important responsibility of expressing God's truth to a spiritually hungry world. We need to let people know what God has done for us and praise God for all that He has done—the "ordinary" as well as the extraordinary.

What specifically can you say that God has done for you?

In what ways have you given Him credit and praise for what He has done?

In what ways have you given the credit to someone or something other than God?

What specific action might you take to become a standing stone for another person—to communicate to him or her what God has done?

closing prayer
I minute

I hope that this lesson has challenged you, as it has me, to be more aware of how close to home Satan really lives. I have also come to realize how very important it is to honor God for what He has done—and is doing—so that our lives can be testimonies for Him.

Dear God, how easy it is for us to turn to Satan's counterfeit offerings instead of to You in order to find meaning and significance in life. How easy it is for us to deny You the credit You deserve. As we live in a culture that isn't so very different from that of Pergamum, open our eyes so that we will be more aware of Satan's influence and can choose to be more faithful to You. Give us the courage to be like Antipas, who remained a faithful witness to the Lord of Lords and King of Kings—Jesus the Messiah. Help us to be like standing stones that remind people of what You've done in the past and what You are doing today. In Your name we pray. Amen.

Evaluate your personal preparedness to refute Satan's false claims:

Which of your personal experiences testify to God being the source of all truth and all blessings?

Which false teachings are you equipped to refute by using the Word of God?

3. *Using the imagery of the white stones inscribed by people who supposedly had been healed by Asclepius, John challenged believers in Pergamum to stand courageously as witnesses for God, telling what He had done in their lives and giving Him the credit He was due.*

Believers today have the important responsibility of expressing God's truth to a spiritually hungry world. We need to let people know what God has done for us and praise God for all that He has done—the "ordinary" as well as the extraordinary.

What specifically can you say that God has done for you?

In what ways have you given Him credit and praise for what He has done?

In what ways have you given the credit to someone or something other than God?

What specific action might you take to become a standing stone for another person—to communicate to him or her what God has done?

PLANNING NOTES:

The Mark of the Beast

Before You Lead

Synopsis

At the beginning of God's message to the Christians living in the prominent city of Ephesus, the apostle John offered words of praise: "I know your deeds, your hard work and your perseverance. . . . You have persevered and have endured hardships for my name, and have not grown weary" (Revelation 2:2–3). These words are remarkable when one considers how challenging it must have been for the early Christians to live and minister in Ephesus. Ray Vander Laan takes his viewers into the ruins of this city to examine the faith of the early Christians who lived there, to discover what gave them the strength to testify of Christ so diligently in such an unlikely place.

The port city of Ephesus, located on what is now the western coast of Turkey, was the crown jewel of Asia Minor. It had a population of nearly 250,000 people and was home to more than twenty pagan temples. Artistic beauty, cultural learning, erotic pagan worship, world trade, criminal activity, and sorcery flourished amidst great opulence. As residents of one of the most sophisticated cities of the Roman Empire, the Ephesians enjoyed such luxuries as running water, indoor toilets, fountains, gardens surrounded by magnificent columns, colonnaded streets paved with marble, gymnasiums and baths, a library, and a theater that could seat an estimated twenty-five thousand people.

At the heart of the city's life and economy was Artemis, the ancient fertility goddess. The temple dedicated to Artemis had more than 120 columns sixty feet high and was one of the seven wonders of the world. Here, priests guarded and protected the purity of Artemis worship for the entire world. Because Artemis was considered to be so powerful and protective of her temple, people from all over the world deposited money there, which in turn was loaned out at a high rate of interest. Thus the Ephesians became extremely wealthy and naturally were very protective of the goddess who had made them successful, powerful, and rich.

Into this city, at the end of his second missionary journey (and also during his third journey), came the apostle Paul. At first he went to the local synagogue, and using the Torah, the prophets, and the life of Jesus the Messiah, he began to teach the Ephesians about the kingdom of God and how they were supposed to live. After several months, he went to a lecture hall of Tyrannus, where every day for two years he spoke the good news of Jesus (Acts 19:9–10). Amazingly, "all the Jews and Greeks who lived in the province of Asia heard the word of the Lord." Most likely, Paul didn't undermine or put down the pagan Ephesians and their beliefs. Rather, he simply and unashamedly spoke God's powerful truth and allowed its implications to impact people.

Of course, the implications of Paul's teaching were huge. The Ephesians realized that if what Paul and other Christians shared was indeed the truth, then Artemis and the other gods of Ephesus were worthless and the city's entire belief system, economy, and lifestyle could collapse. As a result, Paul and other Christians in Ephesus began to face intense opposition. Unless they bore the "mark" of pagan beliefs by living out those beliefs in daily life, Christians were viewed as second-class citizens. They were hated and severely persecuted.

The people's fervor to defend their gods is evident in the accusations of an idol maker named Demetrius, who spread a rumor that Paul believed "that man-made gods are no gods at all" (Acts 19:26). In response, a huge crowd of Artemis worshipers rushed into the theater and chanted "Great is Artemis of the Ephesians!" for about two hours. Finally, fearing the Roman soldiers' response to a riot, the people calmed down and Paul escaped with his life.

Clearly the implications of the truth Paul had spoken so lovingly, so clearly, and so fearlessly had become an offense to unbelievers. Yet the gospel message continued to spread widely as a result of the Christians' bold persistence.

According to tradition, the apostle John also came to Ephesus—in approximately A.D. 70. At that time, John was writing or would soon write the book of Revelation, which includes the message to the church at Ephesus mentioned earlier. By this time, the Roman Emperor Domitian had the upper hand in attracting the religious loyalties of the Ephesians.

Demanding that people worship him as a god, Domitian insisted on being called "Lord" and "God" by everyone, including his wife. The Ephesians built huge structures dedicated to Domitian, including a prominent temple designed to be the world center of Domitian worship. One of its features was a twenty-seven-foot-tall statue of Domitian. Anyone approaching the city by sea or by land could see the temple and its statue and know that the Ephesians as a whole believed Domitian to be king of the gods. Along the city streets, altars reminded the people of Domitian's lordship and their allegiance to him. Once a year, the people had to say publicly in front of an altar, "Caesar is lord." Anyone who didn't recognize Domitian's lordship, including no doubt the early Christians who acknowledged the lordship of God alone, was subject to death.

As Ray points out, it took passionate commitment and courage for the early Christians to stand up for their beliefs in the face of this "mark of the beast." Despite serious persecution, which included the denial to conduct business in the markets and obtain water from the public fountains, the Christians of Ephesus publicly spoke out for Jesus and lived for Him in a loving way. They endured great hardships for Jesus and never became weary of living for Him.

Where did they get the courage and passion to proclaim the gospel in Ephesus? One reason they could work tirelessly for Christ is because of the mutual love and support they demonstrated to one another. When John wrote "You have forsaken your first love" in Revelation 2:4, he was really challenging them to love each other with the love they first had for each other—the love of Jesus. In order to live consistently and publicly for Jesus, they needed to believe in Him and care about each other.

In the final moments of this video, Ray directs viewers to the Pollio Fountain, which was built to remind the Ephesians that the Emperor Domitian was their lord of lords, king of kings, and provider of life. In a similar way, the loving community of Christians was (and still is) to stand in the midst of culture and point people toward God—the true Lord of Lords, King of Kings, and source of life.

As a final reminder, Ray highlights a paving stone unearthed by archaeologists into which symbols of the early church—the "fish" symbol and a cross—had been carved. Somewhere in Ephesus, a person, family, or perhaps an entire community of believers wanted passersby to know, in a quiet and unobtrusive way, that Jesus the Messiah, Son of God, Savior, was Lord of Lords and King of Kings. How will we testify to our world that Jesus is our Lord of Lords and King of Kings?

Key Points of This Lesson

1. In ancient Ephesus, the spiritual battle lines were clearly drawn. Satan offered false gods such as Artemis and the worship of Roman emperors such as Domitian to challenge the lordship of Jesus the Messiah. *In the face of intense persecution, the Ephesian Christians had to choose whom they would serve—and they chose Jesus. They refused to acknowledge the lordship of anyone but God.*

2. *With a passionate, fearless faith in God, Paul and other Christians in Ephesus were unashamed to publicly live out and tirelessly proclaim the truth of God.* Their focus was not to undermine the beliefs of others, but to lovingly, boldly reveal what had been revealed to them. The implications of that truth spoke to people's hearts and minds with such power and conviction that the Bible tells us "all . . . who lived in the province of Asia" heard the gospel message.

3. *The Ephesian believers were known for their love for one another. That love and support helped give them the strength to live consistently, publicly, courageously, and faithfully for Jesus in a city that was openly hostile toward them.*

Session Outline (54 minutes)

I. Introduction (4 minutes)

Welcome

What's to Come

Questions to Think About

II. Show Video "The Mark of the Beast" (27 minutes)

III. Group Discovery (15 minutes)

Video Highlights

Small Group Bible Discovery

IV. Faith Lesson (7 minutes)

Time for Reflection

Action Points

V. Closing Prayer (1 minute)

Materials

No additional materials are needed for this session. Simply view the video prior to leading the session so you are familiar with its main points.

the mark of the beast

introduction

4 minutes

Welcome

> Assemble the participants together. Welcome them to session four of *Faith Lessons on the Early Church.*

What's to Come

In this session, we'll see how the early Christians of Ephesus—a city known for its opulence and worship of false gods, goddesses, and Roman emperors—courageously proclaimed God's lordship and tirelessly spread His message to the world despite intense opposition and persecution. Using the church of Ephesus as a backdrop, Ray Vander Laan explores how important it is for Christians today to live out their faith in public and to proclaim God's truth with persistence, boldness, and passion.

Questions to Think About

> *Participant's Guide page 81.*
> Ask each question and solicit a few responses from group members.

1. What happens when you share your Christian beliefs with non-Christians who are offended by your beliefs? How do you feel and respond when they challenge your faith?

   Suggested Responses: Encourage participants to share their experiences and to be specific about their feelings and responses so that even if they haven't had this experience they will be able to imagine what it could be like and how they might respond. Feelings and responses may include getting angry, taking time to listen and discuss the other people's perspectives, feeling uncomfortable, getting defensive, wanting to prove that your beliefs are superior, wanting to just spend time with Christians, etc.

2. What kinds of situations lead you to become "weary" in your Christian walk? What strengthens or encourages you during those "weary" times?

   Suggested Responses: Encourage participants to consider relationships as well as circumstances. In addition to activities such as reading the Bible, praying, attending church, encourage participants to think of the role other believers play in strengthening each other.

SESSION FOUR

the mark of the beast

questions to think about

1. What happens when you share your Christian beliefs with non-Christians who are offended by your beliefs? How do you feel and respond when they challenge your faith?

2. What kinds of situations lead you to become "weary" in your Christian walk? What strengthens or encourages you during those "weary" times?

3. Imagine that you and a few new believers are the only Christians in your city, that its people don't want you to speak publicly about your faith, and that unless you proclaim allegiance to their view of the world, you will lose your job, you won't be able to buy food, your water and electricity will be shut off, and you might even be killed. What would you do? How would you live?

✏ 3. Imagine that you and a few new believers are the only Christians in your city, that its people don't want you to speak publicly about your faith, and that unless you proclaim allegiance to their view of the world, you will lose your job, you won't be able to buy food, your water and electricity will be shut off, and you might even be killed. What would you do? How would you live?

Suggested Responses: Encourage participants to consider the high personal price that some Christians have to pay if they speak publicly about their faith. Help them to think through the possible consequences to various responses such as speaking out anyway, keeping quiet and hoping no one notices, trying to influence others to support their viewpoint, pretending to give allegiance, etc.

Let's keep these ideas in mind as we view the video.

video presentation
27 minutes

> *Participant's Guide page 82.*

On page 82 of your Participant's Guide, you will find a space in which to take notes on key points as we watch this video.

Leader's Video Observations

Ephesus, Crown Jewel of Asia

Artemis of the Ephesians

Paul Begins to Teach

The Implications of God's Truth

Who Is Lord and God?

A Legacy of Christian Love

the Mark of the Beast

questions to think about

1. What happens when you share your Christian beliefs with non-Christians who are offended by your beliefs? How do you feel and respond when they challenge your faith?

2. What kinds of situations lead you to become "weary" in your Christian walk? What strengthens or encourages you during those "weary" times?

3. Imagine that you and a few new believers are the only Christians in your city, that its people don't want you to speak publicly about your faith, and that unless you proclaim allegiance to their view of the world, you will lose your job, you won't be able to buy food, your water and electricity will be shut off, and you might even be killed. What would you do? How would you live?

82   Faith Lessons on the Early Church

video notes

Ephesus, Crown Jewel of Asia

Artemis of the Ephesians

Paul Begins to Teach

The Implications of God's Truth

Who Is Lord and God?

A Legacy of Christian Love

PLANNING NOTES:

group discovery

15 minutes

> If your group has seven or more members, use the **Video Highlights** with the entire group (5 minutes), then break into small groups of three to five to discuss the **Small Group Bible Discovery** (10 minutes).
>
> If your group has fewer than seven members, begin with the **Video Highlights** (5 minutes), then do one or more of the topics found in the **Small Group Bible Discovery** as a group (10 minutes).

Video Highlights (5 minutes)

> *Here you'll ask one or more of the following questions that directly relate to the video the participants have just seen.*

Asia Minor

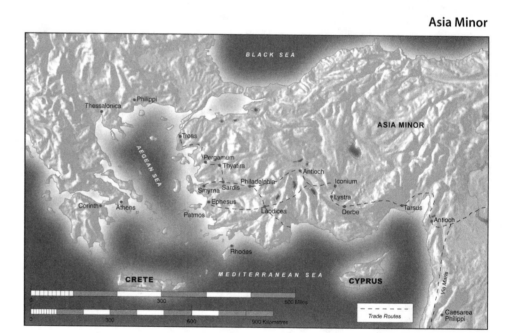

1. Locate Ephesus on the map of Asia Minor above. Why would Ephesus have been an important city even if it hadn't been the world center for the worship of Artemis and the Roman Emperor Domitian?

   Suggested Responses: As an important harbor city, it was on the crossroads of land and sea trade routes between Rome, Egypt, Persia, and the Middle East.

2. What do you imagine it would have been like to live as a Christian in Ephesus?

   Suggested Responses: Encourage participants to put themselves in the place of the Christians in Ephesus and imagine the excitement, fear, and eagerness of standing up for what they believed; the empowerment and courage that came from being part of a loving, supportive, Christian community; the thankfulness and thrill of seeing pagan people turn toward God; etc.

video highlights

1. Locate Ephesus on the map of Asia Minor below. Why would Ephesus have been an important city even if it hadn't been the world center for the worship of Artemis and the Roman Emperor Domitian?

2. What do you imagine it would have been like to live as a Christian in Ephesus?

Asia Minor

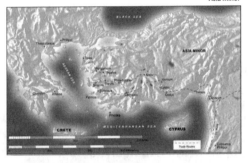

✏ 3. Why do you think God was able to use Paul and the other Christians in Ephesus in such significant ways?

Suggested Responses: Paul and the other Christians knew and believed the Scriptures, kept speaking the good news despite hostility, put God's truth out there and let its implications sink into people's hearts and minds, were willing to stand against the tide of popular opinion for what they knew was true, etc.

✏ 4. What did it mean for the Ephesian Christians to choose who—God or the Roman emperor—was Lord in their lives? What does this suggest to Christians today who desire Christ to be Lord?

Suggested Responses: For the Ephesian Christians, choosing Jesus as Lord meant a total, life-changing (and perhaps a life-giving) commitment. There can be only one "Lord" of our lives. Perhaps Christians today need to reassess their commitment and determine what is required, the choices that must be made, for Christ truly to be Lord of their lives.

Small Group Bible Discovery (10 minutes)

Participant's Guide pages 84–99.

During this time, a group with fewer than seven participants will stay together. A group with seven or more participants will break into small groups. Assign each group one of the following topics. If you have more than four small groups, assign some topics to more than one group.

Let's break into groups of three to five—people sitting near you—and study some of the Bible passages and truths mentioned in the video.

Turn to pages 84–99 in your Participant's Guide. There you'll find a list of four topics. You'll have ten minutes to read and discuss the topic I'll assign to you.

Assign each group a topic.

I'll signal you when one minute is left.

Topic A: Paul's Ministry in Ephesus

As we better understand Paul's ministry in Ephesus, we learn what other early believers there faced and how God used them to spread His message to the world. We also see that the truth of the gospel message always undermines the beliefs of paganism, which often prompts a negative reaction from unbelievers.

✏ 1. Read Acts 19:8–12.

a. Where and for how long did Paul teach in Ephesus?

Suggested Responses: Paul taught first in the synagogue of Ephesus for three months, then he and other believers taught in the Tyrannus lecture hall for two years.

Note: This is the longest known period of time that Paul spent in one location. Even though he remained in Ephesus for an extended time, the impact of his teaching spread to all the Jews and Greeks living in the Roman province of Asia!

3. Why do you think God was able to use Paul and the other Christians in Ephesus in such significant ways?

4. What did it mean for the Ephesian Christians to choose who—God or the Roman emperor—was Lord in their lives? What does this suggest to Christians today who desire Christ to be Lord?

small Group Bible Discovery

Topic A: Paul's Ministry in Ephesus

As we better understand Paul's ministry in Ephesus, we learn what other early believers there faced and how God used them to spread His message to the world. We also see that the truth of the gospel message always undermines the beliefs of paganism, which often prompts a negative reaction from unbelievers.

1. Read Acts 19:8–12.

   a. Where and for how long did Paul teach in Ephesus?

PLANNING NOTES:

    b. What did Paul proclaim in Ephesus, and how did he demonstrate God's power over Satan?

Suggested Responses: Paul proclaimed the kingdom of God, the Word of the Lord. God performed extraordinary miracles through Paul, which demonstrated that God's power was stronger than Satan's power.

2. For which two things was Ephesus famous, and how did the implications of the gospel affect these practices?

    a. Acts 19:18–20

    Suggested Responses: Many people in Ephesus practiced sorcery. When some of these people became believers, they confessed their sins and burned their scrolls publicly.

Note: Ephesus was widely known for the Ephesian Letters, magic charms or amulets that were supposed to bring success, health, and fertility to those who wore them.

    b. Acts 19:23–27

    Suggested Responses: Ephesus was the world center for the worship of Artemis, and there was quite a market for miniature idols of silver, clay, or wood that people could have in their homes. The craftsmen who made these idols realized that large numbers of people were believing the truths of God that Paul proclaimed (one of which was that man-made gods are not gods). If the trend continued, their idol-making businesses could fail, Artemis could lose her worldwide status as a divine goddess, and the lifestyle they had built around the goddess Artemis would disappear.

3. What kind of temple for the true God did exist in Ephesus? (See Ephesians 2:19–22.)

Suggested Responses: The believers themselves, built on the foundation of the apostles and prophets of which Jesus was the chief cornerstone, formed the holy temple of the true God.

b. What did Paul proclaim in Ephesus, and how did he demonstrate God's power over Satan?

2. For which two things was Ephesus famous, and how did the implications of the gospel affect these practices?

a. Acts 19:18–20

b. Acts 19:23–27

3. What kind of temple for the true God did exist in Ephesus? (See Ephesians 2:19–22.)

PLANNING NOTES:

PROFILE OF A MAN-MADE GODDESS
Artemis

Who was Artemis?	The supposed goddess of fertility.
Who worshiped her?	She was probably the most-worshiped deity in Asia and perhaps the world during Paul's time.
What was worship like?	Hundreds of eunuch priests, virgin priestesses, and religious prostitutes served her. Worship rituals were quite erotic.
By what other names was Artemis known?	"Queen of Heaven," "Savior," and "Mother Goddess."
What role did Ephesus have in Artemis worship?	Ephesus was considered *neokorus* for Artemis, which meant the city was the center for Artemis worship and was responsible for maintaining the cult's purity of worship.
How did Ephesus benefit financially from the worship of Artemis?	The cult brought great wealth to the citizens of Ephesus because the temple of Artemis became the world's largest bank during that time.
What were Artemis festivals like?	Devotees came from all over the world to worship and celebrate during her festivals. Huge processions honored her statues. Celebrations were held with music, dancing, singing, dramatic presentations, and chanting of allegiance.
What were Artemis statues like?	They portrayed Artemis as having many breasts —a symbol of her fertility. The main statue in her temple may have been a black meteorite, because she was said to have fallen from the sky.
What was the Artemis temple like?	The temple was one of the seven wonders of the ancient world.
How else do we know that Artemis was important to Ephesus?	Two statues of her have been found in the Prytaneion—the "city hall" of Ephesus— indicating that she was considered to be the basis for life in the city.
What attracted people to Artemis?	The promise of fertility, long life, sexual fulfillment, and protection during pregnancy and childbirth; the seductive sexuality of her worship.

PROFILE OF A MAN-MADE GODDESS: ARTEMIS

Who was Artemis?	The supposed goddess of fertility.
Who worshiped her?	She was probably the most-worshiped deity in Asia and perhaps the world during Paul's time.
What was worship like?	Hundreds of eunuch priests, virgin priestesses, and religious prostitutes served her. Worship rituals were quite erotic.
By what other names was Artemis known?	"Queen of Heaven," "Savior," and "Mother Goddess."
What role did Ephesus have in Artemis worship?	Ephesus was considered *neokorus* for Artemis, which meant the city was the center for Artemis worship and was responsible for maintaining the cult's purity of worship.
How did Ephesus benefit financially from the worship of Artemis?	The cult brought great wealth to the citizens of Ephesus because the temple of Artemis became the world's largest bank during that time.
What were Artemis festivals like?	Devotees came from all over the world to worship and celebrate during her festivals. Huge processions honored her statues. Celebrations were held with music, dancing, singing, dramatic presentations, and chanting of allegiance.
What were Artemis statues like?	They portrayed Artemis as having many breasts—a symbol of her fertility. The main statue in her temple may have been a black meteorite because she was said to have fallen from the sky.
What was the Artemis temple like?	The temple was one of the seven wonders of the ancient world.
How else do we know that Artemis was important to Ephesus?	Two statues of her have been found in the Prytaneion—the "city hall" of Ephesus—indicating that she was considered to be the basis for life in the city.
What attracted people to Artemis?	The promise of fertility, long life, sexual fullfillment, and protection during pregnancy and childbirth; the seductive sexuality of her worship.

DATA FILE

The Theater at Ephesus

In the world of the early believers, the theater was a significant institution for communicating the Hellenistic view of the world. Every major city in the Roman world had a theater, and the theater in Ephesus was spectacular. The Greek king Lysimachus originally built the theater in Ephesus during the third century B.C. Emperor Claudius (A.D. 41–54) enlarged it, and Emperor Nero (A.D. 54–68) continued renovations.

The ruins remaining demonstrate how impressive the theater in Ephesus once was. It had three tiers of seats and could hold an estimated twenty-five thousand people. The stage was 130 feet wide and 80 feet deep. Imagine how the theater must have roared when thousands of devotees of the goddess Artemis became angry at Paul and shouted praises to their goddess for two hours!

Although the stage building is mostly gone, it's interesting to note that the audience in Ephesus preferred no backdrop to the stage. They wanted to see life in the city beyond. The drama that took place on the stage portrayed the way the Ephesians viewed themselves; it was a reflection of their lives. In another sense, the drama portrayed the goal for which the culture was striving—who the people wanted to be. So, the people preferred to look beyond the stage to what was happening in their community.

The Theater at Ephesus

Theaters such as the one in Ephesus were used for both entertainment and religious festivals. Regular plays—dramas (often portraying the myths of the gods), comedies, satires—typically began with sacrifices to Dionysus (the god of theater) and other deities in order to dedicate the presentation to the gods.

During a festival honoring a particular god or goddess, a procession would begin at the god's temple and parade through Ephesus. Led by priests, priestesses, and cult members, the celebrants and pilgrims would carry the symbols and statues of their deity. Passersby would honor the god with gifts or by placing incense on altars placed along the route. The procession typically ended at the theater, where the statues were placed on pedestals and worshiped. People then gave speeches, sacrificed animals, and offered the meat on altars in the stage area. Faithful devotees would then eat the roasted or boiled meat, symbolizing their communion with the deity.

Thus, it became difficult, if not impossible, for Christians in Ephesus to frequent the theater. They would not participate in the sacrifices before dramatic presentations, were offended by stories of gods that the human imagination had created, and refused to eat meat sacrificed to gods that represented demonic powers. No doubt the citizens of Ephesus hated the Christians—not so much for their beliefs but for their refusal to compromise and honor the deities that other people worshiped. As emperor worship became more prevalent, Christians risked their lives to avoid such celebrations.

DATA FILE

The Theater at Ephesus

In the world of the early believers, the theater was a significant institution for communicating the Hellenistic view of the world. Every major city in the Roman world had a theater, and the theater in Ephesus was spectacular. The Greek king Lysimachus originally built the theater in Ephesus during the third century B.C. Emperor Claudius (A.D. 41–54) enlarged it, and Emperor Nero (A.D. 54–68) continued renovations.

The ruins remaining demonstrate how impressive the theater in Ephesus once was. It had three tiers of seats and could hold an estimated twenty-five thousand people. The stage was 130 feet wide and 80 feet deep. Imagine how the theater must have roared when thousands of devotees of the goddess Artemis became angry at Paul and shouted praises to their goddess for two hours!

Although the stage building is mostly gone, it's interesting to note that the audience in Ephesus preferred no backdrop to the stage. They wanted to see life in the city beyond. The drama that took place on the

(continued on page 88)

The Theater at Ephesus

(continued from page 87)

stage portrayed the way the Ephesians viewed themselves; it was a reflection of their lives. In another sense, the drama portrayed the goal for which the culture was striving—who the people wanted to be. So, the people preferred to look beyond the stage to what was happening in their community.

Theaters such as the one in Ephesus were used for both entertainment and religious festivals. Regular plays—dramas (often portraying the myths of the gods), comedies, satires—typically began with sacrifices to Dionysus (the god of theater) and other deities in order to dedicate the presentation to the gods.

During a festival honoring a particular god or goddess, a procession would begin at the god's temple and parade through Ephesus. Led by priests, priestesses, and cult members, the celebrants and pilgrims would carry the symbols and statues of their deity. Passersby would honor the god with gifts or by placing incense on altars placed along the route. The procession typically ended at the theater, where the statues were placed on pedestals and worshiped. People then gave speeches, sacrificed animals, and offered the meat on altars in the stage area. Faithful devotees would then eat the roasted or boiled meat, symbolizing their communion with the deity.

Thus, it became difficult, if not impossible, for Christians in Ephesus to frequent the theater. They would not participate in the sacrifices before dramatic presentations, were offended by stories of gods that the human imagination had created, and refused to eat meat sacrificed to gods that represented demonic powers. No doubt the citizens of Ephesus hated the Christians—not so much for their beliefs but for their refusal to compromise and honor the deities that other people worshiped. As emperor worship became more prevalent, Christians risked their lives to avoid such celebrations.

Topic B: Emperor Worship in Ephesus

Long before the Romans or Paul came to Ephesus, the people of Asia Minor had considered their rulers to be divine. Croesus, king of Sardis (around 550 B.C.), was honored as a divine king. Alexander the Great declared that he was a descendant of Heracles and Zeus and was therefore divine. Inhabitants of the cities he conquered were delighted to consider him a god and honored him with statues, festivals, and regular sacrifices. So the people of Asia Minor did not balk when the Roman Emperors, starting with Caesar Augustus, began making claims to be divine.

As the early Christians began spreading the gospel message throughout Asia Minor, emperor worship was growing rapidly. In Ephesus, Domitian, who was obsessed with his claim to deity, built a huge temple dedicated to himself and enforced his worship under the threat of death. The Ephesians were required to declare Caesar as lord and to sprinkle incense on an altar to indicate their allegiance to him. They were also expected to sacrifice to the emperor and eat sacrificed meat. Severe penalties existed for anyone who refused to publicly acknowledge that Caesar was lord. So Ephesus became a dangerous place for Christians, who would declare no one other than Jesus the Messiah to be Lord.

1. What event concluded Jesus' final forty days on earth after His resurrection? What did this event reveal about Jesus in light of the growing emperor-worship cult? (See Acts 1:1–11.)

   Suggested Responses: Jesus spent forty days on earth, instructing His disciples. At the end of this time, the disciples watched Him ascend into heaven, which demonstrated that He was indeed the Son of God, not like the Roman emperors who merely claimed divinity.

2. In 1 Timothy 1:3, Paul writes that he wants Timothy to stay in Ephesus in order to stand against certain men who taught false doctrine. Based on the points Paul emphasized in 1 Timothy 6:11–16, what might have been the nature of his concern?

   Suggested Responses: No doubt Paul was aware of the growing emperor worship in Ephesus, so he encouraged Timothy to hold onto his faith and the hope of eternal life. In numerous ways, he reminded his coworkers of God's divinity: the blessed and only Ruler, the King of Kings, the Lord of Lords, the only immortal One, the One who lives in incredible glory ("unapproachable light").

3. In what ways does the fact that Roman emperors demanded to be worshiped as "lord" add to the meaning of the following verses?

   a. Romans 10:9

      Suggested Responses: The early Christians had a choice—to say the emperor was "lord" or to say "Jesus is Lord." There was no room for compromise, and to say that Jesus was Lord could mean death. But at the same time, to say that Jesus was Lord meant life—salvation through Christ Jesus whom God had raised from the dead!

   b. Philippians 2:5–11

      Suggested Responses: This is a masterful counter to the claims to deity made by any Roman emperor. Here Paul emphasized that Jesus was "in the very

Topic B: Emperor Worship in Ephesus

Long before the Romans or Paul came to Ephesus, the people of Asia Minor had considered their rulers to be divine. Croesus, king of Sardis (around 550 B.C.), was honored as a divine king. Alexander the Great declared that he was a descendant of Heracles and Zeus and was therefore divine. Inhabitants of the cities he conquered were delighted to consider him a god and honored him with statues, festivals, and regular sacrifices. So the people of Asia Minor did not balk when the Roman Emperors, starting with Caesar Augustus, began making claims to be divine.

As the early Christians began spreading the gospel message throughout Asia Minor, emperor worship was growing rapidly. In Ephesus, Domitian, who was obsessed with his claim to deity, built a huge temple dedicated to himself and enforced his worship under the threat of death. The Ephesians were required to declare Caesar as lord and to sprinkle incense on an altar to indicate their allegiance to him. They were also expected to sacrifice to the emperor and eat sacrificed meat. Severe penalties existed for anyone who refused to publicly acknowledge that Caesar was lord. So Ephesus became a dangerous place for Christians, who would declare no one other than Jesus the Messiah to be Lord.

1. What event concluded Jesus' final forty days on earth after His resurrection? What did this event reveal about Jesus in light of the growing emperor-worship cult? (See Acts 1:1–11.)

2. In 1 Timothy 1:3, Paul writes that he wants Timothy to stay in Ephesus in order to stand against certain men who taught false doctrine. Based on the points Paul emphasized in 1 Timothy 6:11–16, what might have been the nature of his concern?

3. In what ways does the fact that Roman emperors demanded to be worshiped as "lord" add to the meaning of the following verses?

   a. Romans 10:9

   b. Philippians 2:5–11

DID YOU KNOW?

A Roman emperor was declared to be divine when a witness came forward claiming to have seen the emperor ascend to heaven or claiming to have seen the emperor's father ascend to heaven (making the current emperor the "Son of God"). This process was called *apotheosis*.

nature God" and chose to come to earth as a human and die on a cross, for which God exalted Him in heaven. Paul has no doubt that everyone will one day bow to Him and confess that He is Lord. No matter what the Roman emperors or their worshiping followers said, Jesus will one day be acknowledged as Lord!

4. Why was King Herod struck down by God, and what might this event have taught the believers in Ephesus who had to confront emperor worship? (See Acts 12:21–24.)

Suggested Responses: King Herod (Herod Agrippa) received the praises of people in Caesarea who claimed that he was a god and not a man. Because the king didn't defer the praise to God, he was eaten by worms and died. No doubt this was a powerful reminder to the believers that the God they served was the only true God.

5. What was Paul's prayer for the Ephesian believers, who faced persecution from people who worshiped the Roman emperor and other false gods? (See Ephesians 3:14–21.)

Suggested Responses: Paul asked that the believers would be strengthened with power through God's Spirit, rooted and established in love, and have the power to grasp the incredible love of Christ that surpasses knowledge, etc. He ended his prayer by emphasizing the great power of God at work in their lives and glorifying their Lord, Christ Jesus.

DID YOU KNOW?

A Roman emperor was declared to be divine when a witness came forward claiming to have seen the emperor ascend to heaven or claiming to have seen the emperor's father ascend to heaven (making the current emperor the "Son of God"). This process was called *apotheosis*.

FACTS TO CONSIDER

The Demands of Emperor Worship

Every person in Ephesus and other cities that worshiped the emperor was expected to:

- Participate in festivals honoring the emperor(s). This included offering incense on altars carried by priests to declare that Caesar was Lord, making sacrifices to the emperor, and eating sacrificed meat.
- Offer incense to Caesar before entering the city.
- To obey Caesar without question.
- To acknowledge the authority of the emperor when conducting business or shopping in the market. They were to stop at his altars to acknowledge his "lordship," had to acknowledge the emperor as the provider of life before drawing water from public fountains, etc.

2. In 1 Timothy 1:3, Paul writes that he wants Timothy to stay in Ephesus in order to stand against certain men who taught false doctrine. Based on the points Paul emphasized in 1 Timothy 6:11–16, what might have been the nature of his concern?

3. In what ways does the fact that Roman emperors demanded to be worshiped as "lord" add to the meaning of the following verses?

   a. Romans 10:9

   b. Philippians 2:5–11

DID YOU KNOW?

A Roman emperor was declared to be divine when a witness came forward claiming to have seen the emperor ascend to heaven or claiming to have seen the emperor's father ascend to heaven (making the current emperor the "Son of God"). This process was called *apotheosis*.

4. Why was King Herod struck down by God, and what might this event have taught the believers in Ephesus who had to confront emperor worship? (See Acts 12:21–24.)

5. What was Paul's prayer for the Ephesian believers, who faced persecution from people who worshiped the Roman emperor and other false gods? (See Ephesians 3:14–21.)

FACTS TO CONSIDER

The Demands of Emperor Worship

Every person in Ephesus and other cities that worshiped the emperor was expected to:

- Participate in festivals honoring the emperor(s). This included offering incense on altars carried by priests to declare that Caesar was Lord, making sacrifices to the emperor, and eating sacrificed meat.
- Offer incense to Caesar before entering the city.
- To obey Caesar without question.
- To acknowledge the authority of the emperor when conducting business or shopping in the market. They were to stop at his altars to acknowledge his "lordship," had to acknowledge the emperor as the provider of life before drawing water from public fountains, etc.

PLANNING NOTES:

DATA FILE

The Temple of Domitian

Temple of Domitian

Built on the slope of the hill south of Ephesus and extending into the center of the city, this prominent temple could be seen from nearly everywhere in Ephesus, including the land and harbor entrances. The Ephesians, who built it to honor their emperor in order to gain the greatest benefits from him, pressured other Ephesians and the province of Asia Minor to declare the emperor "Lord and God."

Huge columns more than thirty-five feet high supported the two-hundred-by-three-hundred-foot podium on which the temple of Domitian rested. One unusual feature is that these columns had carvings that represented various deities. Apparently the Ephesians designed the podium this way in order to declare that the emperor was supported by all the world's gods and that he was the culmination of all deity— the final lord of heaven and earth, the god of gods.

Although not large, the forty-by-sixty-foot temple had four columns in the front and a row of columns around the outside (eight in front and back, thirteen on the sides). A large, marble altar stood on a raised platform and had a U-shaped colonnade around it with the open end facing the temple. On altars such as this one, the people were required to sprinkle incense to declare that Caesar was lord.

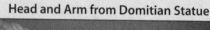

Head and Arm from Domitian Statue

A statue of what is believed to be Domitian stood near the temple and altar. Based on the huge arm and head that have been excavated, researchers believe the statue was twenty-seven feet tall. After Domitian died, he was discredited by the Roman senate, and the temple was rededicated to his beloved father, Vespasian, who was emperor from A.D. 69–79. Today, the ruins reveal the emperors' great earthly glory and also declare the futility of denying the lordship of the God of the Bible.

DATA FILE

The Temple of Domitian

Built on the slope of the hill south of Ephesus and extending into the center of the city, this prominent temple could be seen from nearly everywhere in Ephesus, including the land and harbor entrances. The Ephesians, who built it to honor their emperor in order to gain the greatest benefits from him, pressured other Ephesians and the province of Asia Minor to declare the emperor "Lord and God."

Huge columns more than thirty-five feet high supported the two-hundred-by-three-hundred-foot podium on which the temple of Domitian rested. One unusual feature is that these columns had carvings that represented various deities. Apparently the Ephesians designed the podium this way in order to declare that the emperor was supported by all the world's gods and that he was the culmination of all deity—the final lord of heaven and earth, the god of gods.

Although not large, the forty-by-sixty-foot temple had four columns in the front and a row of columns around the outside (eight in front and back, thirteen on the sides). A large, marble altar stood on a raised platform and had a U-shaped colonnade around it with the open end facing the temple. On altars such as this one, the people were required to sprinkle incense to declare that Caesar was lord.

Temple of Domitian

A statue of what is believed to be Domitian stood near the temple and altar. Based on the huge arm and head that have been excavated, researchers believe the statue was twenty-seven feet tall. After Domitian died, he was discredited by the Roman senate, and the temple was rededicated to his beloved father, Vespasian, who was emperor from A.D. 69–79. Today, the ruins reveal the emperors' great earthly glory and also declare the futility of denying the lordship of the God of the Bible.

Head and Arm from Domitian Statue

Topic C: Living as Witnesses in an Evil Culture

With a population of nearly 250,000 and a reputation for being the richest city in the world, Ephesus was a trend-setting place—not unlike New York City or Los Angeles today. Its seaport, which provided a key link in the Roman world between the east (Persia, Syria, Judea, Egypt) and the west (Greece, Rome), made it a center of political and commercial power. Ephesus was a stronghold of Satanic power as well. People came from all over the world to worship the goddess Artemis, many people were demon possessed, people practiced magic and sorcery, and emperor worship was celebrated. Despite these seeming obstacles, the gospel message found fertile ground in this powerful, pagan city.

1. What did God do to demonstrate His power over evil in Ephesus? (See Acts 19:11–12.)

Topic C: Living as Witnesses in an Evil Culture

With a population of nearly 250,000 and a reputation for being the richest city in the world, Ephesus was a trend-setting place—not unlike New York City or Los Angeles today. Its seaport, which provided a key link in the Roman world between the east (Persia, Syria, Judea, Egypt) and the west (Greece, Rome), made it a center of political and commercial power. Ephesus was a stronghold of Satanic power as well. People came from all over the world to worship the goddess Artemis, many people were demon possessed, people practiced magic and sorcery, and emperor worship was celebrated. Despite these seeming obstacles, the gospel message found fertile ground in this powerful, pagan city.

1. What did God do to demonstrate His power over evil in Ephesus? (See Acts 19:11–12.)

   Suggested Responses: God did miracles through Paul, such as healing the sick and demon-possessed people who simply touched handkerchiefs and aprons that had touched Paul. Clearly this communicated that God's power was stronger than Satan's.

2. People in Ephesus were fascinated by the power Paul wielded as he accomplished God's work. Read Acts 19:13–20 to discover the impact God's power had on the people of Ephesus.

   a. Which event terrified the Jews and Greeks who lived in Ephesus? Why do you think this terrified them?

      Suggested Responses: Some Jews, who evidently were not believers, sought to imitate Paul by invoking the name of Jesus in order to cast out demons from a man. But the evil spirit questioned who they were, and then the demon-possessed man beat them up badly and sent them running for their lives. This incident caused unbelievers to hold the name of Jesus in high esteem.

   b. What impact did this incident have on Ephesian believers who had been dabbling in sorcery?

      Suggested Responses: They were convicted of their sin and publicly repented. They burned their scrolls, which were worth a great deal of money.

3. In contrast to their pagan neighbors, how were the Ephesian believers to live? (See Ephesians 5:8–12, 15–20.)

   Suggested Responses: They were to live as "children of light"; to demonstrate goodness, righteousness, and truth; to discover what pleases the Lord; to avoid evil deeds of spiritual darkness and expose evil for what it was; to live wisely; to use every God-given opportunity; to know the Lord's will; to be filled with the Holy Spirit; to sing and make music to the Lord; to give thanks to the Lord for everything; etc.

4. At the end of his letter to the Ephesian believers, Paul offers advice on how they could continue to live for God in the face of great evil. Read Ephesians 6:10–18 and answer the following questions.

A statue of what is believed to be Domitian stood near the temple and altar. Based on the huge arm and head that have been excavated, researchers believe the statue was twenty-seven feet tall. After Domitian

Head and Arm from Domitian Statue

died, he was discredited by the Roman senate, and the temple was rededicated to his beloved father, Vespasian, who was emperor from A.D. 69–79. Today, the ruins reveal the emperors' great earthly glory and also declare the futility of denying the lordship of the God of the Bible.

Topic C: Living as Witnesses in an Evil Culture

With a population of nearly 250,000 and a reputation for being the richest city in the world, Ephesus was a trend-setting place—not unlike New York City or Los Angeles today. Its seaport, which provided a key link in the Roman world between the east (Persia, Syria, Judea, Egypt) and the west (Greece, Rome), made it a center of political and commercial power. Ephesus was a stronghold of Satanic power as well. People came from all over the world to worship the goddess Artemis, many people were demon possessed, people practiced magic and sorcery, and emperor worship was celebrated. Despite these seeming obstacles, the gospel message found fertile ground in this powerful, pagan city.

1. What did God do to demonstrate His power over evil in Ephesus? (See Acts 19:11–12.)

2. People in Ephesus were fascinated by the power Paul wielded as he accomplished God's work. Read Acts 19:13–20 to discover the impact God's power had on the people of Ephesus.

   a. Which event terrified the Jews and Greeks who lived in Ephesus? Why do you think this terrified them?

   b. What impact did this incident have on Ephesian believers who had been dabbling in sorcery?

3. In contrast to their pagan neighbors, how were the Ephesian believers to live? (See Ephesians 5:8–12, 15–20.)

4. At the end of his letter to the Ephesian believers, Paul offers advice on how they could continue to live for God in the face of great evil. Read Ephesians 6:10–18 and answer the following questions.

a. Who did Paul say the believers were really fighting as they shared the gospel message? (See verses 10–12.)

Suggested Responses: They were not doing battle with people. They were fighting Satan's schemes—battling the rulers, authorities, and powers of darkness on earth and the evil spiritual forces in heavenly realms.

b. How did Paul say the Ephesian believers could stand their ground? (See verse 13.)

Suggested Response: by putting on the full armor of God so they could combat Satan's schemes.

DATA FILE

The Sign of the Fish—*ixthus*

Early Christian believers often used the "fish" symbol. This may be because Jesus called His disciples to be "fishers of men" (Matthew 4:19). Or, perhaps the Greek word for fish, *ixthus*, was an acrostic for Jesus Christ, Son of God, Savior:

i—first letter in the Greek word for "Jesus"

x—first letter in the Greek word for "Christ"

th—first letter in the Greek word for "God"

u—first letter in the Greek word for "son"

s—first letter in the Greek word for "savior"

WORTH OBSERVING . . .

Called to Pursue Our "First Love"

According to Matthew 22:37–38, believers in Jesus the Messiah are to love the Lord their God with all their heart, soul, and mind (strength). Yet, according to Romans 13:8–10, 1 John 2:9–11, 1 John 3:10–11, and other biblical passages, love for other people is the preeminent sign that a person loves God. Thus, as believers, we are called to love other people. This is the first love that occurs when one is in relationship with God.

Love, in fact, distinguishes the community of God's people from people who do not love God. When Paul wrote to the Ephesian believers (probably around A.D. 54), he mentioned their love for one another (Ephesians 1:15–16) and encouraged loving unity in the body of Christ (Ephesians 4:15–16). Their love for one another is perhaps one reason the church in Ephesus had such an impact in such an evil place. But later, God warned the Ephesians that they had forsaken their "first love" (Revelation 2:1–7). This implies that they may have become divided over theological issues.

Unfortunately, many Christians today focus more on their disagreements than they do on simply loving one another. Could that be one reason why the church as a whole is so fractured today, why our witness for Jesus has been greatly weakened, and why the Christian community as a whole is not as effective today as it was in Ephesus?

a. Who did Paul say the believers were really fighting as they shared the gospel message? (See verses 10–12.)

b. How did Paul say the Ephesian believers could stand their ground? (See verse 13.)

DATA FILE

The Sign of the Fish—*ixthus*

Early Christian believers often used the "fish" symbol. This may be because Jesus called His disciples to be "fishers of men" (Matthew 4:19). Or, perhaps the Greek word for fish, *ixthus*, was an acrostic for Jesus Christ, Son of God, Savior:

i—first letter in the Greek word for "Jesus"
x—first letter in the Greek word for "Christ"
th—first letter in the Greek word for "God"
u—first letter in the Greek word for "son"
s—first letter in the Greek word for "savior"

WORTH OBSERVING . . .

Called to Pursue Our "First Love"

According to Matthew 22:37–38, believers in Jesus the Messiah are to love the Lord their God with all their heart, soul, and mind (strength). Yet, according to Romans 13:8–10, 1 John 2:9–11, 1 John 3:10–11, and other biblical passages, love for other people is the preeminent sign that a person loves God. Thus, as believers, we are called to love other people. This is the first love that occurs when one is in relationship with God.

Love, in fact, distinguishes the community of God's people from people who do not love God. When Paul wrote to the Ephesian believers (probably around A.D. 54), he mentioned their love for one another (Ephesians 1:15–16) and encouraged loving unity in the body of Christ (Ephesians 4:15–16). Their love for one another is perhaps one reason the church in Ephesus had such an impact in such an evil place. But later, God warned the Ephesians that they had forsaken their "first love" (Revelation 2:1–7). This implies that they may have become divided over theological issues.

Unfortunately, many Christians today focus more on their disagreements than they do on simply loving one another. Could that be one reason why the church as a whole is so fractured today, why our witness for Jesus has been greatly weakened, and why the Christian community as a whole is not as effective today as it was in Ephesus?

Topic D: *Chutzpah*

The apostles were so persistent in teaching and living out Jesus' message because they were totally convinced that Jesus was the Messiah and He had prepared them well to carry His message to the world. But there is another reason they were so effective, and that has to do with their understanding of their faith.

In the Jewish culture of that time, the word *faith* had many meanings. One meaning was "bold persistence, unyielding intensity that will not give up." That's what the Hebrew word *chutzpah* meant. Thus, the early believers were bold, determined, persistent, and unwilling to

---

PLANNING NOTES:

Topic D: *Chutzpah*

The apostles were so persistent in teaching and living out Jesus' message because they were totally convinced that Jesus was the Messiah and He had prepared them well to carry His message to the world. But there is another reason they were so effective, and that has to do with their understanding of their faith.

In the Jewish culture of that time, the word *faith* had many meanings. One meaning was "bold persistence, unyielding intensity that will not give up." That's what the Hebrew word *chutzpah* meant. Thus, the early believers were bold, determined, persistent, and unwilling to be stopped in their service to God. (It did not mean they were to be overly pushy, negatively aggressive, or disrespectful toward anyone, which is a connotation the word has in our culture.) Let's consider how the Jewish understanding of faith helped spread the gospel to the world.

1. According to the following verses, what was the early Christians' (including those in Ephesus) fundamental source of boldness?

Scripture	Source of *Chutzpah*
2 Timothy 1:6–7	*the Spirit of power, love, and self-discipline that God provided*
Acts 1:8	*the Holy Spirit who gave them power to be Jesus' witnesses*
Acts 4:29–31	*the Holy Spirit who empowered them to speak boldly and gave them the ability to do miracles*

2. According to Luke 11:5–8, why did the man finally receive the bread he needed? What did Jesus teach about *chutzpah* through this parable?

   Suggested Responses: The man kept boldly asking, refusing to give up. Likewise, we are to persistently ask God for what we need.

3. How did Abraham demonstrate *chutzpah* in Genesis 18:16–33?

   Suggested Responses: He talked with God about the judgment that would be poured on Sodom and Gomorrah. He kept negotiating with God about how few righteous people had to live in those cities in order for God to spare the cities. He refused to give up until God agreed to spare the cities if ten righteous people lived in them.

4. In Ephesus, a key center of idol worship, how did Paul demonstrate *chutzpah*? (See Acts 19:8–10; Ephesians 6:19–20.)

   Suggested Responses: Paul boldly spoke the truth of God daily to the Ephesians, first in the synagogue and then in a lecture hall. He wanted to be fearless for Jesus, regardless of the consequences to his life.

WORTH OBSERVING . . .

Called to Pursue Our "First Love"

According to Matthew 22:37–38, believers in Jesus the Messiah are to love the Lord their God with all their heart, soul, and mind (strength). Yet, according to Romans 13:8–10, 1 John 2:9–11, 1 John 3:10–11, and other biblical passages, love for other people is the preeminent sign that a person loves God. Thus, as believers, we are called to love other people. This is the first love that occurs when one is in relationship with God.

Love, in fact, distinguishes the community of God's people from people who do not love God. When Paul wrote to the Ephesian believers (probably around A.D. 54), he mentioned their love for one another (Ephesians 1:15–16) and encouraged loving unity in the body of Christ (Ephesians 4:15–16). Their love for one another is perhaps one reason the church in Ephesus had such an impact in such an evil place. But later, God warned the Ephesians that they had forsaken their "first love" (Revelation 2:1–7). This implies that they may have become divided over theological issues.

Unfortunately, many Christians today focus more on their disagreements than they do on simply loving one another. Could that be one reason why the church as a whole is so fractured today, why our witness for Jesus has been greatly weakened, and why the Christian community as a whole is not as effective today as it was in Ephesus?

Topic D: *Chutzpah*

The apostles were so persistent in teaching and living out Jesus' message because they were totally convinced that Jesus was the Messiah and He had prepared them well to carry His message to the world. But there is another reason they were so effective, and that has to do with their understanding of their faith.

In the Jewish culture of that time, the word *faith* had many meanings. One meaning was "bold persistence, unyielding intensity that will not give up." That's what the Hebrew word *chutzpah* meant. Thus, the early believers were bold, determined, persistent, and unwilling to

be stopped in their service to God. (It did not mean they were to be overly pushy, negatively aggressive, or disrespectful toward anyone, which is a connotation the word has in our culture.) Let's consider how the Jewish understanding of faith helped spread the gospel to the world.

1. According to the following verses, what was the early Christians' (including those in Ephesus) fundamental source of boldness?

Scripture	Source of *Chutzpah*
2 Timothy 1:6–7	
Acts 1:8	
Acts 4:29–31	

2. According to Luke 11:5–8, why did the man finally receive the bread he needed? What did Jesus teach about *chutzpah* through this parable?

3. How did Abraham demonstrate *chutzpah* in Genesis 18:16–33?

4. In Ephesus, a key center of idol worship, how did Paul demonstrate *chutzpah*? (See Acts 19:8–10; Ephesians 6:19–20.)

DID YOU KNOW?

People *Will* Respond to God's Truth

The Word of God is true, and we can confidently share the gospel message with anyone. But God's truth is also powerful and it *will* make an impact—at times it will turn people's hearts toward God and at other times it will bring us into conflict with people who deny God's truth.

Situation	What Happened
Peter shared God's truth with the crowd at Pentecost (Acts 2:14–41).	About three thousand people received God's truth and became Christians.
Peter and John healed a beggar and shared the gospel message with people near the temple in Jerusalem (Acts 3–4:4; 4:18–21).	The religious leaders seized Peter and John and threw them into prison; about five thousand men who heard God's truth became Christians. The leaders then commanded Peter and John to stop preaching; they refused and were let go.
Philip preached God's truth to the followers of Simon the Sorcerer (Acts 8:9–13).	Simon and many of his followers became believers and were baptized.
Paul and Barnabas preached in Pisidian Antioch to almost the entire city (Acts 13:42–52).	Jealous Jews attacked what Paul was saying, Paul and Silas boldly answered them, and God's Word spread throughout the entire region. Paul and Barnabas were then expelled from the region.

DID YOU KNOW?

People *Will* Respond to God's Truth

The Word of God is true, and we can confidently share the gospel message with anyone. But God's truth is also powerful and it *will* make an impact—at times it will turn people's hearts toward God and at other times it will bring us into conflict with people who deny God's truth.

Situation	What Happened
Peter shared God's truth with the crowd at Pentecost (Acts 2:14–41).	About three thousand people received God's truth and became Christians.
Peter and John healed a beggar and shared the gospel message with people near the temple in Jerusalem (Acts 3–4:4; 4:18–21).	The religious leaders seized Peter and John and threw them into prison; about five thousand men who heard God's truth became Christians. The leaders then commanded Peter and John to stop preaching; they refused and were let go.
Philip preached God's truth to the followers of Simon the Sorcerer (Acts 8:9–13).	Simon and many of his followers became believers and were baptized.
Paul and Barnabas preached in Pisidian Antioch to almost the entire city (Acts 13:42–52).	Jealous Jews attacked what Paul was saying, Paul and Silas boldly answered them, and God's Word spread throughout the entire region. Paul and Barnabas were then expelled from the region.
Paul and Silas boldly preached in the Jewish temple in Iconium for quite a long time (Acts 14:1–7).	Many Jews and Gentiles became believers, but unbelieving Jews stirred up the people. Finally, upon learning that they were to be killed, Paul and Silas left the city and preached in other places.
After casting an evil spirit out of a girl, Paul and Silas were thrown into prison, where they prayed and sang hymns to God. After God delivered them from prison, they preached to the jailer and his household (Acts 16:16–34).	The jailer and all his family became believers and were baptized.
Paul spoke to the Corinthians in the house of Titius Justus and kept on teaching the Word of God for a year and a half (Acts 18:7–17).	The synagogue ruler in Corinth, his entire household, and many Corinthians became believers. The Jews took Paul to court, complaining that he was causing people to worship God in ways contrary to the law. The case was thrown out of court.

4. In Ephesus, a key center of idol worship, how did Paul demonstrate *chutzpah*? (See Acts 19:8–10; Ephesians 6:19–20.)

DID YOU KNOW?

People *Will* Respond to God's Truth

The Word of God is true, and we can confidently share the gospel message with anyone. But God's truth is also powerful and it *will* make an impact—at times it will turn people's hearts toward God and at other times it will bring us into conflict with people who deny God's truth.

Situation	What Happened
Peter shared God's truth with the crowd at Pentecost (Acts 2:14–41).	About three thousand people received God's truth and became Christians.
Peter and John healed a beggar and shared the gospel message with people near the temple in Jerusalem (Acts 3–4:4; 4:18–21).	The religious leaders seized Peter and John and threw them into prison; about five thousand men who heard God's truth became Christians. The leaders then commanded Peter and John to stop preaching; they refused and were let go.
Philip preached God's truth to the followers of Simon the Sorcerer (Acts 8:9–13).	Simon and many of his followers became believers and were baptized.
Paul and Barnabas preached in Pisidian Antioch to almost the entire city (Acts 13:42–52).	Jealous Jews attacked what Paul was saying, Paul and Silas boldly answered them, and God's Word spread throughout the entire region. Paul and Barnabas were then expelled from the region.

Paul and Silas boldly preached in the Jewish temple in Iconium for quite a long time (Acts 14:1–7).	Many Jews and Gentiles became believers, but unbelieving Jews stirred up the people. Finally, upon learning that they were to be killed, Paul and Silas left the city and preached in other places.
After casting an evil spirit out of a girl, Paul and Silas were thrown into prison, where they prayed and sang hymns to God. After God delivered them from prison, they preached to the jailer and his household (Acts 16:16–34).	The jailer and all his family became believers and were baptized.
Paul spoke to the Corinthians in the house of Titius Justus and kept on teaching the Word of God for a year and a half (Acts 18:7–17).	The synagogue ruler in Corinth, his entire household, and many Corinthians became believers. The Jews took Paul to court, complaining that he was causing people to worship God in ways contrary to the law. The case was thrown out of court.

THE TRUTH OF THE MATTER:

The Importance of Acknowledging Jesus as Lord

As the early church grew, believers had two choices: (1) to go along with the pagan world in order to not create offense and endanger themselves and their families; or (2) to stand firm and declare that Jesus was Lord and risk suffering—even death. The witness of the believers was a declaration of war on the Roman state and its Satanic foundation. Here, two worldviews competed for domination of the world, and there could be no compromise.

Today, believers face a similar choice. Will they totally submit to the Lordship of Jesus regardless of the cost? Will they serve Him everywhere and in everything, whether the cost is economic, social, or even life itself? Jesus is Lord. The battle is not between believers and pagan authorities. Rather, it is between Jesus and Satan, and the outcome of that battle has already been determined. (See Revelation 20.)

PLANNING NOTES:

> ## THE TRUTH OF THE MATTER
>
> ### The Importance of Acknowledging Jesus as Lord
>
> As the early church grew, believers had two choices: (1) to go along with the pagan world in order to not create offense and endanger themselves and their families; or (2) to stand firm and declare that Jesus was Lord and risk suffering—even death. The witness of the believers was a declaration of war on the Roman state and its Satanic foundation. Here, two worldviews competed for domination of the world, and there could be no compromise.
>
> Today, believers face a similar choice. Will they totally submit to the Lordship of Jesus regardless of the cost? Will they serve Him everywhere and in everything, whether the cost is economic, social, or even life itself? Jesus is Lord. The battle is not between believers and pagan authorities. Rather, it is between Jesus and Satan, and the outcome of that battle has already been determined. (See Revelation 20.)

> Signal the groups when one minute remains so that they may wrap up their discovery time.

faith Lesson

7 minutes

Time for Reflection (4 minutes)

It's time for each of us to think quietly about how we can live out and proclaim the gospel message to our world. On page 100 of the Participant's Guide, you'll find a passage of Scripture. Let's each read this passage silently and take the next few minutes to consider some of the questions that follow.

Please do not talk during this time. It's a time when we can reflect on today's lesson and how it applies to our lives.

> The Scripture passage and questions are reproduced in their entirety in the Participant's Guide on page 100.

Finally, be strong in the Lord and in his mighty power. Put on the full armor of God so that you can take your stand against the devil's schemes. . . . Pray also for me, that whenever I open my mouth, words may be given me so that I will fearlessly make known the mystery of the gospel, for which I am an ambassador in chains. Pray that I may declare it fearlessly, as I should. (Ephesians 6:10–11, 19–20)

Christians today generally think of the apostle Paul as being fearless—the boldest of the bold—in proclaiming the message of Jesus the Messiah. Yet as he closes his letter to the Ephesians, he asks them to pray that he will be fearless

Paul and Silas boldly preached in the Jewish temple in Iconium for quite a long time (Acts 14:1–7).	Many Jews and Gentiles became believers, but unbelieving Jews stirred up the people. Finally, upon learning that they were to be killed, Paul and Silas left the city and preached in other places.
After casting an evil spirit out of a girl, Paul and Silas were thrown into prison, where they prayed and sang hymns to God. After God delivered them from prison, they preached to the jailer and his household (Acts 16:16–34).	The jailer and all his family became believers and were baptized.
Paul spoke to the Corinthians in the house of Titius Justus and kept on teaching the Word of God for a year and a half (Acts 18:7–17).	The synagogue ruler in Corinth, his entire household, and many Corinthians became believers. The Jews took Paul to court, complaining that he was causing people to worship God in ways contrary to the law. The case was thrown out of court.

THE TRUTH OF THE MATTER:

The Importance of Acknowledging Jesus as Lord

As the early church grew, believers had two choices: (1) to go along with the pagan world in order to not create offense and endanger themselves and their families; or (2) to stand firm and declare that Jesus was Lord and risk suffering—even death. The witness of the believers was a declaration of war on the Roman state and its Satanic foundation. Here, two worldviews competed for domination of the world, and there could be no compromise.

Today, believers face a similar choice. Will they totally submit to the Lordship of Jesus regardless of the cost? Will they serve Him everywhere and in everything, whether the cost is economic, social, or even life itself? Jesus is Lord. The battle is not between believers and pagan authorities. Rather, it is between Jesus and Satan, and the outcome of that battle has already been determined. (See Revelation 20.)

faith lesson

Time for Reflection

Read the following passage of Scripture and take the next few minutes to consider the ways in which you can live out and proclaim the gospel message to your world.

> Finally, be strong in the Lord and in his mighty power. Put on the full armor of God so that you can take your stand against the devil's schemes. . . . Pray also for me, that whenever I open my mouth, words may be given me so that I will fearlessly make known the mystery of the gospel, for which I am an ambassador in chains. Pray that I may declare it fearlessly, as I should.
>
> EPHESIANS 6:10–11, 19–20

Christians today generally think of the apostle Paul as being fearless—the boldest of the bold—in proclaiming the message of Jesus the Messiah. Yet as he closes his letter to the Ephesians, he asks them to pray that he will be fearless in proclaiming the gospel. What does that tell you about Paul and what it takes to truly live for Jesus in an evil world?

As you consider your life and the way in which God has called you to live out and proclaim His truth, for what do you need the prayers of others?

Who can you ask to pray for you in this way?

For whom can you pray for in this way?

Consider the Christians throughout the world who are being persecuted for their faith. What can you do to educate yourself concerning the nature of that persecution so that you can pray for their needs as they seek to "stand against the devil's schemes"?

Action Points

Take a moment to jot down an action step (or steps) that you will commit to this week as a result of what you have learned.

in proclaiming the gospel. What does that tell you about Paul and what it takes to truly live for Jesus in an evil world?

As you consider your life and the way in which God has called you to live out and proclaim His truth, for what do you need the prayers of others?

Who can you ask to pray for you in this way?

For whom can you pray for in this way?

Consider the Christians throughout the world who are being persecuted for their faith. What can you do to educate yourself concerning the nature of that persecution so that you can pray for their needs as they seek to "stand against the devil's schemes"?

Action Points (3 minutes)

The following points are reproduced on pages 100–102 of the Participant's Guide:

Now it's time to wrap up our session.

Give participants a moment to transition from their thoughtfulness to giving you their full attention.

I'd like to take a moment to summarize the key points we explored. After I have reviewed these points, I will give you a moment to jot down an action step (or steps) that you will commit to this week as a result of what you have learned today.

Read the following points and pause afterward so that participants can consider and write out their commitment.

1. In ancient Ephesus, the spiritual battle lines were clearly drawn. Satan offered false gods such as Artemis and the worship of Roman emperors such as Domitian to challenge the lordship of Jesus the Messiah. *In the face of intense persecution, the Ephesian Christians had to choose whom they would serve—and they chose Jesus. They refused to acknowledge the lordship of anyone but God.*

   What powers or idols challenge the lordship of Christ in your life?

   If Christ is anything less than Lord of your life, what steps will you take to restore Him to His rightful place?

2. *With a passionate, fearless faith in God, Paul and other Christians in Ephesus were unashamed to publicly live out and tirelessly proclaim the truth of God.* Their focus was not to undermine the beliefs of others, but to lovingly and boldly reveal what had been revealed to them. The implications of that truth spoke to people's hearts and minds with such power and conviction that the Bible tells us "all . . . who lived in the province of Asia" heard the gospel message.

faith Lesson

Time for Reflection

Read the following passage of Scripture and take the next few minutes to consider the ways in which you can live out and proclaim the gospel message to your world.

> Finally, be strong in the Lord and in his mighty power. Put on the full armor of God so that you can take your stand against the devil's schemes. . . . Pray also for me, that whenever I open my mouth, words may be given me so that I will fearlessly make known the mystery of the gospel, for which I am an ambassador in chains. Pray that I may declare it fearlessly, as I should.
>
> EPHESIANS 6:10–11, 19–20

Christians today generally think of the apostle Paul as being fearless—the boldest of the bold—in proclaiming the message of Jesus the Messiah. Yet as he closes his letter to the Ephesians, he asks them to pray that he will be fearless in proclaiming the gospel. What does that tell you about Paul and what it takes to truly live for Jesus in an evil world?

As you consider your life and the way in which God has called you to live out and proclaim His truth, for what do you need the prayers of others?

Who can you ask to pray for you in this way?

For whom can you pray for in this way?

Consider the Christians throughout the world who are being persecuted for their faith. What can you do to educate yourself concerning the nature of that persecution so that you can pray for their needs as they seek to "stand against the devil's schemes"?

Action Points

Take a moment to jot down an action step (or steps) that you will commit to this week as a result of what you have learned.

1. In ancient Ephesus, the spiritual battle lines were clearly drawn. Satan offered false gods such as Artemis and the worship of Roman emperors such as Domitian to challenge the lordship of Jesus the Messiah. *In the face of intense persecution, the Ephesian Christians had to choose whom they would serve—and they chose Jesus. They refused to acknowledge the lordship of anyone but God.*

   What powers or idols challenge the lordship of Christ in your life?

   If Christ is anything less than Lord of your life, what steps will you take to restore Him to His rightful place?

2. *With a passionate, fearless faith in God, Paul and other Christians in Ephesus were unashamed to publicly live out and tirelessly proclaim the truth of God.* Their focus was not to undermine the beliefs of others, but to lovingly and boldly reveal what had been revealed to them. The implications of that truth spoke to people's hearts and minds with such power and conviction that the Bible tells us "all . . . who lived in the province of Asia" heard the gospel message.

   What one thing have you learned from the early believers' bold and persistent determination to speak out for Jesus that will help you in your efforts to share Jesus with the world around you?

PLANNING NOTES:

What one thing have you learned from the early believers' bold and persistent determination to speak out for Jesus that will help you in your efforts to share Jesus with the world around you?

In what ways do the words *boldness, courage, passion, fearlessness, hard work, faith,* and *perseverance* characterize your public Christian life? What must you do so that they will be more descriptive of your life?

3. *The Ephesian believers were known for their love for one another. That love and support helped give them the strength to live consistently, publicly, courageously, and faithfully for Jesus in a city that was openly hostile toward them.*

In what way(s) might you become more committed to a community of believers who need your love and support and will love and encourage you so that together you can proclaim the kingdom of God?

closing prayer

I minute

I hope that this lesson has challenged you, as it has me, to remember that each of us has a stand to make for God. He will provide what we need in order to live boldly for Him and to proclaim His truth to a spiritually needy world.

Dear God, thank You for the opportunity to share Your truth with people around us. Please help us to recognize the spiritual battle lines in our world so that we can choose You as our Lord. Help us to be bold, persistent, and tireless in sharing Your message with the people around us. We don't want to be apathetic or complacent; we want to be used by You, just like You used the early Christians in Ephesus. Please fill us with Your Spirit and prepare us to stand firm in the face of whatever opposition we will encounter. Open our hearts to love and support one another as we seek to live faithfully for You in an evil world. In Your name we pray, Jesus. Amen.

In what ways do the words *boldness, courage, passion, fearlessness, hard work, faith,* and *perseverance* characterize your public Christian life? What must you do so that they will be more descriptive of your life?

3. *The Ephesian believers were known for their love for one another. That love and support helped give them the strength to live consistently, publicly, courageously, and faithfully for Jesus in a city that was openly hostile toward them.*

    In what way(s) might you become more committed to a community of believers who need your love and support and will love and encourage you so that together you can proclaim the kingdom of God?

PLANNING NOTES:

Hot or cold

Before You Lead

Synopsis

In this session, Ray Vander Laan will explore three ancient cities—Hierapolis, Colosse, and Laodicea—clustered near the Lycus River of Asia Minor. In the book of Revelation, John recorded God's prophetic words to the church in Laodicea: "I know your deeds, that you are neither cold nor hot. I wish you were either one or the other! So, because you are lukewarm—neither hot nor cold—I am about to spit you out of my mouth" (Revelation 3:15–16). An understanding of the geography, and particularly the water sources, of these neighboring cities gives us a new understanding of what this message may have meant to the church of Laodicea and what it means for Christians today.

Hierapolis, known for its healing hot springs, was about six miles from Laodicea. What is left of the entrance to the city—a gate complex of two gigantic towers and three arches that opened onto a paved street about a mile and a half long—stands as a testimony to the city's former majesty. What is most important to this study is not the gate's size or architecture, however, but what it represented.

Like most city gates of the ancient world, the gates of Hierapolis expressed the people's devotion to their deities or rulers. For Hierapolis, that god was the Roman emperor Domitian—one of the first emperors to declare himself to be divine. Thus anyone who entered the Domitian Gate was in a sense acknowledging that Domitian was god—their provider and protector whom they would honor and obey above all others.

Obviously, the early believers who lived in Hierapolis had to choose to serve and worship Caesar (in this case, Domitian) or to serve and worship the God of Israel. According to ancient church tradition, an early missionary named Philip, who most likely was Philip the disciple of Jesus, refused to recognize the authority of Domitian. Philip and his children stood fast in their declaration that Jesus alone is Lord of Lords and King of Kings, and they paid the ultimate price. High on a hill overlooking Hierapolis are the remains of a small building known as the Martyrium of Philip.

Hierapolis was also the site of the Apollo Temple and Plutonium, where the god of music, prophecy, and light was worshiped. Inside the temple, a grand fountain called Nymphia was a constant reminder to the people that Apollo was supposed to be their source of life. Next to the temple was a mysterious hole in the ground known as the Plutonium, the Devil's Hole, or the Gates of Hades. It was believed to be an entrance to the Underworld where Pluto (Latin) or Hades (Greek) lived. Poisonous gases emanated from the hole and instantly killed any animals that wandered in. But the priests of Apollo, who apparently held their breath or had some other means of breathing fresh air, amazed the people by going into the hole and coming out again unharmed—seeming to have power over death.

Another prominent feature of Hierapolis was its theater, which communicated through its architecture as well as its activities the people's devotion to their gods and goddesses. One can still see the images of gods and goddesses depicted in the ornately carved stones. By far the most impressive feature of Hierapolis was its hot springs. The baths of Hierapolis were among the largest in all of Asia Minor, allowing hundreds of people to bathe at the same time. People from distant regions came to soak in warm baths and seek healing for arthritis, skin diseases, and even abdominal problems.

In contrast to Hierapolis, the ancient city of Colosse was known for its cold water. Located about eleven miles from Laodicea, Colosse was built at the foot of Mt. Cadmus, which towered more than nine thousand feet high. Colosse was known for a purple dye called colissinus and for its many, ice-cold snow- and rain-fed streams that rushed down from the snow-covered peak of Mt. Cadmus. People in the fertile Lycus River Valley commonly talked about this wonderful, invigorating water.

Founded several hundreds of years before Hierapolis, Colosse's inhabitants worshiped many gods, including Artemis, Athena, and Demeter. The city was in serious decline by the time of Paul and John because of the growth of Laodicea and Hierapolis. It is known by Christians today because Paul wrote a letter to the Colossians, which was the home of his friend, Philemon, and his slave, Onesimus.

During the first century, the city of Laodicea was the richest and most powerful of the three cities. Located in the Lycus River Valley on the main trade route between the Mediterranean region and Persia, Laodicea was known for its soft, black wool that was appreciated throughout the Roman world; its healing eye salve; and its banking. In fact, an ancient writer recorded that the city of approximately 120,000 people refused an emperor's offer to rebuild following an earthquake. The Laodiceans apparently told the emperor that they were rich and didn't need his money!

Despite its prosperity, however, Laodicea had a serious problem. Its water, unlike the healing hot springs of Hierapolis or the fresh, cold mountain water of Colosse, was lukewarm and full of minerals. It tasted so bad it made people sick.

Ray explains that in light of the water for which the cities of Hierapolis, Laodicea, and Colosse were known, the apostle John might have been saying, "If you were hot, like the springs in Hierapolis, you'd bring healing, restoration, and comfort to people who suffer. If you were cold, like the water in Colosse, you'd refresh and encourage people who are hurting. Instead, you are lukewarm. You don't do anybody any good, and you make me sick—just like your own water." So he challenges Christians today to be hot *and* cold in our daily lives—to bring people the healing, caring, encouraging touch of Jesus.

Ray also urges viewers to be aware of how God prepares people to receive His message and to make the most of the opportunities He has provided. He uses as his example two earthquakes, one in A.D. 17 and one in A.D. 60, that destroyed Laodicea before the gospel arrived. Because of these disasters, the people's faith in their pagan gods wavered. *Zeus, Apollo, Domitian, and Demeter didn't save us,* they thought, *so who will?* They were searching for someone who could fill the gap. So the message of Jesus the Messiah took root in fertile ground. And it appears the believers of Laodicea took John's warning to heart: the church of Laodicea remained a dynamic community after most of the churches of Asia Minor had disappeared.

Key Points of This Lesson

1. *John, when writing to the church in Laodicea, used images of the Laodiceans' everyday world in order to communicate God's message.* He referred to what the Laodiceans had told the Roman emperor who wanted to help them rebuild their city. He mentioned blindness to a city whose key industry was making and marketing eye salve. And he described their faith in terms of the local water—the most basic necessity of life.

2. *God longs for those who follow Him to be wholehearted and passionate in offering His message to a hurting world.* Like the water of Colosse, which was cold, fresh, and invigorating, followers of Christ offer a message that is refreshing to hearts that are weary of sin. Like the warm, healing mineral waters of Hierapolis, followers of Christ offer a message that brings healing to those who are wounded and broken by sin. And like the nauseating, tepid water of Laodicea, followers who do nothing, who are neither hot nor cold, turn God's stomach.

3. *Using what Jesus had taught them, or what they had learned through other believers, early Christians such as Philip passionately proclaimed the gospel throughout the Roman world. Consequently, God used them to change that world!* Christians today have no less of an opportunity to live as Jesus' *talmidim* and bring His message to a lost and hurting world.

Session Outline (52 minutes)

I. Introduction (5 minutes)
Welcome
What's to Come
Questions to Think About

II. Show Video "Hot or Cold" (21 minutes)

III. Group Discovery (16 minutes)
Video Highlights
Small Group Bible Discovery

IV. Faith Lesson (9 minutes)
Time for Reflection
Action Points

V. Closing Prayer (1 minute)

Materials

No additional materials are needed for this session. However, you may want a chalkboard, marker board, or overhead projector to record responses to the **Questions to Think About** so that participants may view them during the Faith Lesson. Please view the video prior to leading the session so you are familiar with its main points.

Hot or cold

introduction

5 minutes

Welcome

> Assemble the participants together. Welcome them to session five of *Faith Lessons on the Early Church.*

What's to Come

Writing the words of God to the church in Laodicea, John stated that the believers were "neither hot nor cold," and that God was ready to spit them out of His mouth. This session explores the history and geography of Laodicea and its neighboring cities—Colosse and Hierapolis—in order to discover what those words may have meant to the believers there. It's a strong encouragement to evaluate our commitment as *talmidim* and to bring the loving, healing, refreshing touch of Jesus to the world around us.

Questions to Think About

> *Participant's Guide page 103.*
>
> Ask each question and solicit a few responses from group members. If desired, write the answers to these questions on a chalkboard, marker board, or overhead projector so that participants may refer to them during the Faith Lesson.

1. Which historical, geographic, or common cultural experiences could you use to help a nonbeliever in your community understand some aspect of the gospel message, or to encourage another believer in his or her walk with God?

   Suggested Responses: Encourage participants to think of things that are unique to their region or lifestyle. For instance, near the ocean, one could imagine one's sins being cast into the deepest sea; one could compare Satan's attacks on believers to ongoing terrorism conducted by a defeated foe; etc.

2. Think about people who have had the greatest influence on your life for Jesus. What was it about them that touched you deeply?

   Suggested Responses: These will vary but are likely to include the person's love, the way the person responded to my needs, the fact that the person cared about me and my world, the person's sacrifices for me, etc.

SESSION FIVE

HOT or cold

Questions to Think About

1. Which historical, geographic, or common cultural experiences could you use to help a nonbeliever in your community understand some aspect of the gospel message, or to encourage another believer in his or her walk with God?

2. Think about people who have had the greatest influence on your life for Jesus. What was it about them that touched you deeply?

3. If you were to go out and make a difference, change the world, and impact your culture for Jesus, how would you go about doing it?

4. If Jesus were to show up at your doorstep tomorrow morning, in what way(s) do you think He'd invite you to reach out to people in your community?

PLANNING NOTES:

✏ 3. If you were to go out and make a difference, change the world, and impact your culture for Jesus, how would you go about doing it?

Suggested Responses: These may vary greatly. Encourage participants to write these down and reconsider them at the close of the session.

✏ 4. If Jesus were to show up at your doorstep tomorrow morning, in what way(s) do you think He'd invite you to reach out to people in your community?

Suggested Responses: These will vary but may include visiting sick people in their homes, handing out food at a food pantry, giving money to a stranded traveler, loaning Christian books to shut-ins, leading a Bible study for prison inmates, inviting non-Christians over for dinner, etc.

Let's keep these ideas in mind as we view the video.

video presentation

21 minutes

> Participant's Guide page 104.

On page 104 of your Participant's Guide, you will find a space in which to take notes on key points as we watch this video.

Leader's Video Observations

Hierapolis

The Domitian Gate

The Theater

The Apollo Temple and Plutonium

The Baths

Colosse and Its Water

Laodicea and Its Water

Changing the World by Being Hot *and* Cold

SESSION FIVE

Hot or Cold

Questions to Think About

1. Which historical, geographic, or common cultural experiences could you use to help a nonbeliever in your community understand some aspect of the gospel message, or to encourage another believer in his or her walk with God?

2. Think about people who have had the greatest influence on your life for Jesus. What was it about them that touched you deeply?

3. If you were to go out and make a difference, change the world, and impact your culture for Jesus, how would you go about doing it?

4. If Jesus were to show up at your doorstep tomorrow morning, in what way(s) do you think He'd invite you to reach out to people in your community?

Video Notes

Hierapolis

    The Domitian Gate

    The Theater

    The Apollo Temple and Plutonium

    The Baths

Colosse and Its Water

Laodicea and Its Water

Changing the World by Being Hot *and* Cold

Group Discovery

16 minutes

> If your group has seven or more members, use the **Video Highlights** with the entire group (6 minutes), then break into small groups of three to five to discuss the **Small Group Bible Discovery** (10 minutes).
>
> If your group has fewer than seven members, begin with the **Video Highlights** (6 minutes), then do one or more of the topics found in the **Small Group Bible Discovery** as a group (10 minutes).

Video Highlights (6 minutes)

> *Here you'll ask one or more of the following questions that directly relate to the video the participants have just seen.*

✎ 1. Locate the cities of Laodicea, Hierapolis, and Colosse on the map of Asia Minor and the Lycus River Valley on page 106 of your participant's guide. Note that Hierapolis is six miles and Colosse is eleven miles away from Laodicea. What surprised you about these cities?

Suggested Responses: These will vary but may include differences in gods and worship, how different they were for being in such close proximity, how they rose and fell in prominence, differences in population, etc.

✎ 2. When you first heard John's words to the Laodicean church, what did you think the terms "hot" and "cold" meant?

Suggested Responses: These may vary, but most likely will be similar to the following: "hot" meant to enthusiastically serve God, obey Him, communicate His message, live out His truth; "cold" meant to not live God's way, to not pray or read the Bible regularly, to not respond to people's needs, etc.

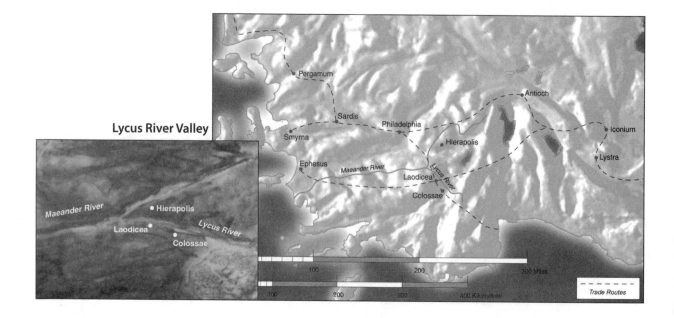

Lycus River Valley

video Highlights

1. Locate the cities of Laodicea, Hierapolis, and Colosse on the map of Asia Minor and the Lycus River Valley on page 106 of your participant's guide. Note that Hierapolis is six miles and Colosse is eleven miles away from Laodicea. What surprised you about these cities?

2. When you first heard John's words to the Laodicean church, what did you think the terms "hot" and "cold" meant?

3. In what ways does the possibility that a Christian should be both "hot" *and* "cold" change your perspective?

4. If you had been a Christian living in Hierapolis, what choices might you have had to make on a daily basis in order to live out and proclaim the gospel message?

5. What do you think enabled disciples such as Philip to be successful in proclaiming the gospel and changing the world of Asia Minor?

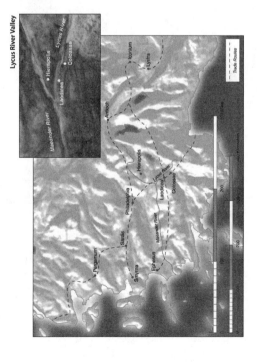

Lycus River Valley

PLANNING NOTES:

✏ 3.   In what ways does the possibility that a Christian should be both "hot" *and* "cold" change your perspective?

Suggested Responses: These will vary. Give participants some time to consider the implications.

✏ 4.   If you had been a Christian living in Hierapolis, what choices might you have had to make on a daily basis in order to live out and proclaim the gospel message?

Suggested Responses: will vary but may include whether or not to go through the gates or to get water from the fountain in the Apollo Temple, whether or not to participate in the theater, enjoy the baths, etc.

✏ 5.   What do you think enabled disciples such as Philip to be successful in proclaiming the gospel and changing the world of Asia Minor?

Suggested Response: They had observed Jesus' method for changing the lives of people, which is to demonstrate His love in practical ways; they had seen Him ascend to heaven and knew without a doubt that He was the Son of God; they were totally committed to being His *talmidim*, meaning they would faithfully obey and wholeheartedly seek to be like Him.

DATA FILE

If This Theater Could Talk

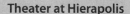

Theater at Hierapolis

The first-century theater of Hierapolis, one of the best-preserved theaters in Asia, clearly demonstrates the city's sophistication at the time Epaphras founded a church there. The carvings below the stage, which was twelve feet high, are in remarkable condition. They depict the mythology of Apollo and Artemis and clearly show the connection between the theater and the worship of pagan gods. This particular theater had seating for seventeen thousand spectators, and in the center of the seating area was a "royal box" from which dignitaries watched events.

The Greeks and Romans considered the theater to be more than entertainment. It displayed the ideals of the Hellenistic culture, communicating to people that "This is who we are, and this is who we should become." That's why Greek theaters such as this one were built so that the audience could see the actors on the stage against the backdrop of their communities.

For Christians of that day, the theater created a dilemma. There was nothing inherently sinful about drama, nor were all the presentations there an insult to godly values. But as an institution, the theater presented a seductive argument for the pagan lifestyle. The plays were dedicated to the gods before they began and were used to shape the values and beliefs of those who aspired to be all that a Greek or Roman should be.

video нighlights

1. Locate the cities of Laodicea, Hierapolis, and Colosse on the map of Asia Minor and the Lycus River Valley on page 106 of your participant's guide. Note that Hierapolis is six miles and Colosse is eleven miles away from Laodicea. What surprised you about these cities?

2. When you first heard John's words to the Laodicean church, what did you think the terms "hot" and "cold" meant?

3. In what ways does the possibility that a Christian should be both "hot" *and* "cold" change your perspective?

4. If you had been a Christian living in Hierapolis, what choices might you have had to make on a daily basis in order to live out and proclaim the gospel message?

5. What do you think enabled disciples such as Philip to be successful in proclaiming the gospel and changing the world of Asia Minor?

DATA FILE

If This Theater Could Talk

The first-century theater of Hierapolis, one of the best-preserved theaters in Asia, clearly demonstrates the city's sophistication at the time Epaphras founded a church there. The carvings below the stage, which was twelve feet high, are in remarkable condition. They depict the mythology of Apollo and Artemis and clearly show the connection between the theater and the worship of pagan gods. This particular theater had seating for seventeen thousand spectators, and in the center of the seating area was a "royal box" from which dignitaries watched events.

Theater at Hierapolis

The Greeks and Romans considered the theater to be more than entertainment. It displayed the ideals of the Hellenistic culture, communicating to people that "This is who we are, and this is who we should become." That's why Greek theaters such as this one were built so that the audience could see the actors on the stage against the backdrop of their communities.

For Christians of that day, the theater created a dilemma. There was nothing inherently sinful about drama, nor were all the presentations there an insult to godly values. But as an institution, the theater presented a seductive argument for the pagan lifestyle. The plays were dedicated to the gods before they began and were used to shape the values and beliefs of those who aspired to be all that a Greek or Roman should be.

TIMELINE OF EVENTS IN AND AROUND ASIA MINOR

2000–1000 B.C.	Hittite Empire
920–586 B.C.	Divided kingdom of Israel
586 B.C.	Babylonian captivity
500 B.C.	Jews' return from captivity
325 B.C.	Alexander the Great's conquest
261 B.C.	Laodicea founded
220 B.C.	Antiochus settles Jews from Babylon in Asia
133 B.C.	Roman Empire begins; lasts until A.D. 300
27 B.C.-A.D. 14	Augustus
A.D. 37–41	Caligula (enforced emperor worship)
@ A.D. 48–49	Paul's third missionary journey (Ephesus)
@ A.D. 60	Paul is martyred
A.D. 60	Earthquake damages Laodicea, Hierapolis, and Colosse
@ A.D. 68–78	John is in Asia
A.D. 81–96	Domitian/emperor worship in Ephesus
A.D. 90–100	The book of Revelation written between these dates
A.D. 98–117	Trajan
@ A.D. 110	John's death
@ A.D. 325	Christianity becomes state religion
A.D. 363	A significant church council held in Laodicea

Small Group Bible Discovery (10 minutes)

Participant's Guide pages 109–20.

During this time, a group with fewer than seven participants will stay together. A group with seven or more participants will break into small groups. Assign each group one of the following topics. If you have more than five small groups, assign some topics to more than one group.

Let's break into groups of three to five—people sitting near you—and study some of the Bible passages and truths mentioned in the video.

Turn to pages 109–20 in your Participant's Guide. There you'll find a list of five topics. You'll have ten minutes to read and discuss the topic I'll assign to you.

Assign each group a topic.

I'll signal you when one minute is left.

108   Faith Lessons on the Early Church

Timeline of Events in and around Asia Minor

2000–1000 B.C.	Hittite Empire
920–586 B.C.	Divided kingdom of Israel
586 B.C.	Babylonian captivity
500 B.C.	Jews' return from captivity
325 B.C.	Alexander the Great's conquest
261 B.C.	Laodicea founded
220 B.C.	Antiochus settles Jews from Babylon in Asia
133 B.C.	Roman Empire begins; lasts until A.D. 300
27 B.C.–A.D. 14	Augustus
A.D. 37–41	Caligula (enforced emperor worship)
@ A.D. 48–49	Paul's second missionary journey (Ephesus)
@ A.D. 60	Paul is martyred
A.D. 60	Earthquake damages Laodicea, Hierapolis, and Colosse
@ A.D. 68–78	John is in Asia
A.D. 81–96	Domitian/emperor worship in Ephesus
A.D. 90–100	The book of Revelation written between these dates
A.D. 98–117	Trajan
@ A.D. 110	John's death
@ A.D. 325	Christianity becomes state religion
A.D. 363	A significant church council held in Laodicea

Session Five: Hot or Cold   109

small group bible discovery

Topic A: Faithful *Talmidim*

God provides opportunities for His followers to witness for Him. To be a *talmid* means to be prepared and committed to respond to those opportunities and to be faithful in trusting God to provide the right words and actions. Based on church history, it appears that Philip—one of Jesus' disciples—was God's messenger in Hierapolis. We also know from the Bible that Epaphras, another determined follower of Jesus, probably founded the churches of Laodicea, Hierapolis, and Colosse.

1. What do the following verses reveal about Philip's commitment to being a *talmid* of Jesus?

Scripture	Philip, *talmid* of Jesus the Rabbi
Mark 3:13–19	
John 1:43–49	
John 12:20–22	

2. Read John 6:1–14 and 14:6–14. In what ways would these two situations have prepared Philip for his later ministry?

Topic A: Faithful *Talmidim*

God provides opportunities for His followers to witness for Him. To be a *talmid* means to be prepared and committed to respond to those opportunities and to be faithful in trusting God to provide the right words and actions. Based on church history, it appears that Philip—one of Jesus' disciples—was God's messenger in Hierapolis. We also know from the Bible that Epaphras, another determined follower of Jesus, probably founded the churches of Laodicea, Hierapolis, and Colosse.

1. What do the following verses reveal about Philip's commitment to being a *talmid* of Jesus?

Scripture	Philip, *talmid* of Jesus the Rabbi
Mark 3:13–19	*Philip was one of Jesus' twelve disciples. As such, he spent three years with Jesus being prepared for ministry.*
John 1:43–49	*Philip came from the small town of Bethsaida and followed Jesus immediately. He spoke so knowledgeably and boldly about Jesus that skeptical Nathanael came to meet Jesus and recognized Him as the Messiah.*
John 12:20–22	*Evidently Philip was recognized as a disciple and was approachable because Gentiles asked him to work things out so they could meet Jesus.*

2. Read John 6:1–14 and 14:6–14. In what ways would these two situations have prepared Philip for his later ministry?

   Suggested Responses: In both incidents, Jesus addressed Philip specifically. In the feeding of the 5,000 Jesus provided food miraculously, in a way Philip apparently could not have imagined. In the second, Jesus probed Philip's belief in Jesus as the Messiah. He provided strong assurance that He was indeed the Son of God, sent to do the work of the Father. In both incidents, Philip no doubt recognized anew that Jesus was indeed the Messiah, and that what He said was true.

3. What do the following passages reveal about Epaphras and his work on behalf of the gospel?

Scripture	Epaphras, faithful messenger of the gospel
Colossians 1:1–8	*Epaphras faithfully proclaimed the gospel in Colosse and evidently helped to lead the new church there. He was also Paul's friend and stayed in touch with him.*
Philemon 23	*Because of his stand for Jesus, Epaphras was imprisoned with Paul.*
Colossians 4:12–13	*Epaphras, who served the Colossian Christians and Jesus, was a prayer warrior who "wrestled" in prayer for the struggling new church in Colosse. He worked hard for the churches in Colosse, Laodicea, and Hierapolis.*

small Group Bible Discovery

Topic A: Faithful *Talmidim*

God provides opportunities for His followers to witness for Him. To be a *talmid* means to be prepared and committed to respond to those opportunities and to be faithful in trusting God to provide the right words and actions. Based on church history, it appears that Philip—one of Jesus' disciples—was God's messenger in Hierapolis. We also know from the Bible that Epaphras, another determined follower of Jesus, probably founded the churches of Laodicea, Hierapolis, and Colosse.

1. What do the following verses reveal about Philip's commitment to being a *talmid* of Jesus?

Scripture	Philip, *talmid* of Jesus the Rabbi
Mark 3:13–19	
John 1:43–49	
John 12:20–22	

2. Read John 6:1–14 and 14:6–14. In what ways would these two situations have prepared Philip for his later ministry?

110   Faith Lessons on the Early Church

3. What do the following passages reveal about Epaphras and his work on behalf of the gospel?

Scripture	Epaphras, faithful messenger of the gospel
Colossians 1:1–8	
Philemon 23	
Colossians 4:12–13	

THE TRUTH OF THE MATTER

Confronting the Hellenism of Today

"Man," said the Greek philosopher Protagoras (481–411 B.C.), "is the measure of all things of what is and what is not." This philosophy provided the foundation for Hellenism, which was devoted to the supremacy of human beings and human accomplishment. The cultural tradition of the Greeks, Hellenism was the prevalent worldview before and during the growth of early Christianity.

Hellenism was based on the belief that human beings are the ultimate source of truth and authority in the universe. Since the human being was considered the "measure of all," human wisdom was deemed to be the greatest wisdom. What could not be understood or explained was viewed as false. Human accomplishments in athletics, the arts, and architecture became the motivating drive of society. The human body was considered the ultimate in beauty, so nudity in art, in the baths, and in sport was common. The accumulation of material possessions in order to provide oneself with luxury and comfort was a common pursuit. What could be more natural than to get the most out of life? After all, life's greatest goal was to be the best at any pursuit.

THE TRUTH OF THE MATTER

Confronting the Hellenism of Today

"Man," said the Greek philosopher Protagoras (481–411 B.C.), "is the measure of all things of what is and what is not." This philosophy provided the foundation for Hellenism, which was devoted to the supremacy of human beings and human accomplishment. The cultural tradition of the Greeks, Hellenism was the prevalent worldview before and during the growth of early Christianity.

Hellenism was based on the belief that human beings are the ultimate source of truth and authority in the universe. Since the human being was considered the "measure of all," human wisdom was deemed to be the greatest wisdom. What could not be understood or explained was viewed as false. Human accomplishments in athletics, the arts, and architecture became the motivating drive of society. The human body was considered the ultimate in beauty, so nudity in art, in the baths, and in sport was common. The accumulation of material possessions in order to provide oneself with luxury and comfort was a common pursuit. What could be more natural than to get the most out of life? After all, life's greatest goal was to be the best at any pursuit.

The Hellenists tried to build their society on their gods, which were human creations. In effect, they worshiped themselves. Because they had nothing greater than themselves on which to base their worldview and society, their society eventually collapsed. No society can exist for very long when it creates its own view of truth.

Was Hellenism, at its roots, really new? No. The first evidence of it is recorded when Satan asked Eve, "Did God really say . . . ?" (see Genesis 3:1). Eve, and then Adam, faced an earth-shaking choice: who, or what, was the ultimate source of truth in the universe? When Adam and Eve decided to disobey God's command not to eat from the tree (Genesis 2:16–17), they decided for themselves what was right and best for them and didn't depend on God. They crowned themselves as the ultimate authority in the universe.

In contrast, the worldview of Christianity is based on God as the ultimate truth and authority. His revelation is the source of our vision for society, our knowledge, our morality, and even truth itself. The resulting values are absolute—not merely creations of our imaginations—and form a strong basis for society and the belief in the dignity of each person who is created in God's image. In such a worldview, God is the ultimate authority in the universe. Life is to be lived for Him, not for ourselves. God has created the ultimate in beauty, not humankind. Truth is what God has revealed and allowed people to discover.

The core beliefs of Hellenism haven't disappeared with the advancements of today's culture. Today Hellenism is called Humanism, and it still promotes the idea that the human being is the ultimate authority in the universe. Thus truth is what the human mind can discover, demonstrate, and understand. The glorification of human accomplishment, the drive to be number one, the obsession with comfort and pleasure, the focus on the human body and sexuality, the lack of compassion for other people, and the commitment to the will of the majority as being right are built on a foundation that is as old as the Garden of Eden and was well articulated by ancient Greek philosophers.

Today we commonly hear such phrases as: "Just do it." "If it feels good, who can tell you it's wrong for you?" "I have the right to choose what to do with my body." Within our public educational system, Hellenistic teaching is prevalent. Truth is defined as that which each person can logically understand and demonstrate (or at least that which the majority of people decides is right).

What does this mean to believers today? We live in the same type of world as the early Christian missionaries did. Our great task, then, is to declare that God alone is supreme and to obey Him. Our great temptation is that we may compromise and live as Hellenists or Humanists—and lose the opportunity to bring God's life-transforming love and truth to a spiritually needy world.

3. What do the following passages reveal about Epaphras and his work on behalf of the gospel?

Scripture	Epaphras, faithful messenger of the gospel
Colossians 1:1–8	
Philemon 23	
Colossians 4:12–13	

THE TRUTH OF THE MATTER

Confronting the Hellenism of Today

"Man," said the Greek philosopher Protagoras (481–411 B.C.), "is the measure of all things of what is and what is not." This philosophy provided the foundation for Hellenism, which was devoted to the supremacy of human beings and human accomplishment. The cultural tradition of the Greeks, Hellenism was the prevalent worldview before and during the growth of early Christianity.

Hellenism was based on the belief that human beings are the ultimate source of truth and authority in the universe. Since the human being was considered the "measure of all," human wisdom was deemed to be the greatest wisdom. What could not be understood or explained was viewed as false. Human accomplishments in athletics, the arts, and architecture became the motivating drive of society. The human body was considered the ultimate in beauty, so nudity in art, in the baths, and in sport was common. The accumulation of material possessions in order to provide oneself with luxury and comfort was a common pursuit. What could be more natural than to get the most out of life? After all, life's greatest goal was to be the best at any pursuit.

The Hellenists tried to build their society on their gods, which were human creations. In effect, they worshiped themselves. Because they had nothing greater than themselves on which to base their worldview and society, their society eventually collapsed. No society can exist for very long when it creates its own view of truth.

Was Hellenism, at its roots, really new? No. The first evidence of it is recorded when Satan asked Eve, "Did God really say . . . ?" (see Genesis 3:1). Eve, and then Adam, faced an earth-shaking choice: who, or what, was the ultimate source of truth in the universe? When Adam and Eve decided to disobey God's command not to eat from the tree (Genesis 2:16–17), they decided for themselves what was right and best for them and didn't depend on God. They crowned themselves as the ultimate authority in the universe.

In contrast, the worldview of Christianity is based on God as the ultimate truth and authority. His revelation is the source of our vision for society, our knowledge, our morality, and even truth itself. The resulting values are absolute—not merely creations of our imaginations—and form a strong basis for society and the belief in the dignity of each person who is created in God's image. In such a worldview, God is the ultimate authority in the universe. Life is to be lived for Him, not for ourselves. God has created the ultimate in beauty, not humankind. Truth is what God has revealed and allowed people to discover.

The core beliefs of Hellenism haven't disappeared with the advancements of today's culture. Today Hellenism is called Humanism, and it still promotes the idea that the human being is the ultimate authority in the universe. Thus truth is what the human mind can discover, demonstrate, and understand. The glorification of human accomplishment, the drive to be number one, the obsession with comfort and pleasure, the focus on the human body and sexuality, the lack of compassion for other people, and the commitment to the will of the majority as being right are built on a foundation that is as old as the Garden of Eden and was well articulated by ancient Greek philosophers.

Today we commonly hear such phrases as: "Just do it." "If it feels good, who can tell you it's wrong for you?" "I have the right to choose what to

(continued on page 112)

(continued from page 111)

do with my body." Within our public educational system, Hellenistic teaching is prevalent. Truth is defined as that which each person can logically understand and demonstrate (or at least that which the majority of people decides is right).

What does this mean to believers today? We live in the same type of world as the early Christian missionaries did. Our great task, then, is to declare that God alone is supreme and to obey Him. Our great temptation is that we may compromise and live as Hellenists or Humanists—and lose the opportunity to bring God's life-transforming love and truth to a spiritually needy world.

Topic B: Called to Be a Healing Influence

In the world of the early church, hot baths were a key source of health care. People sought healing by bathing or ingesting the hot, mineral-filled water of Hierapolis. John's metaphor of "hot" (Revelation 3:15) was probably drawn from these baths, which could be seen from Laodicea.

1. What did Jesus promise His followers would do? (See John 14:12.)

2. What does James 5:13–16 reveal about the power of Christ's followers to bring about healing?

Topic B: Called to Be a Healing Influence

In the world of the early church, hot baths were a key source of health care. People sought healing by bathing or ingesting the hot, mineral-filled water of Hierapolis. John's metaphor of "hot" (Revelation 3:15) was probably drawn from these baths, which could be seen from Laodicea.

1. What did Jesus promise His followers would do? (See John 14:12.)

   Suggested Response: If they had faith in Him, Jesus' followers would be able to do what Jesus had been doing—and even greater things. This included healing and other miracles.

2. What does James 5:13–16 reveal about the power of Christ's followers to bring about healing?

   Suggested Responses: Someone who is sick should ask the church elders to pray over him (or her) and anoint him with oil in the name of the Lord. The confession of sins and prayer for one another brings about forgiveness and healing.

3. What is the nature and source of the gift of healing, and why is it given? (See 1 Corinthians 12:7–12, 27–28.)

   Suggested Responses: God, through the Holy Spirit, provides all gifts, including the gift of healing. Every believer, as part of the body of Christ, has a specific gift that is determined by God. Clearly some believers were to do healing, just as Jesus had done.

4. Read Matthew 25:31–46 and write down six types of healing in which believers are to be involved.

   Suggested Responses: providing food for hungry people, a drink for thirsty people, shelter for strangers, clothing for those who need clothes, caring for people who are sick, and visiting people in prison.

5. What other kinds of healing do believers provide, according to the following verses?

   a. Colossians 3:12–13

      Suggested Response: Believers are to conduct themselves with compassion, kindness, humility, gentleness, patience, and forgiveness—all of which bring healing to other people.

   b. 2 Corinthians 1:3–5

      Suggested Response: Because God comforts them, believers are to comfort other people.

(continued from page 111)

do with my body." Within our public educational system, Hellenistic teaching is prevalent. Truth is defined as that which each person can logically understand and demonstrate (or at least that which the majority of people decides is right).

What does this mean to believers today? We live in the same type of world as the early Christian missionaries did. Our great task, then, is to declare that God alone is supreme and to obey Him. Our great temptation is that we may compromise and live as Hellenists or Humanists—and lose the opportunity to bring God's life-transforming love and truth to a spiritually needy world.

Topic B: Called to Be a Healing Influence

In the world of the early church, hot baths were a key source of health care. People sought healing by bathing or ingesting the hot, mineral-filled water of Hierapolis. John's metaphor of "hot" (Revelation 3:15) was probably drawn from these baths, which could be seen from Laodicea.

1. What did Jesus promise His followers would do? (See John 14:12.)

2. What does James 5:13–16 reveal about the power of Christ's followers to bring about healing?

3. What is the nature and source of the gift of healing, and why is it given? (See 1 Corinthians 12:7–12, 27–28.)

4. Read Matthew 25:31–46 and write down six types of healing in which believers are to be involved.

5. What other kinds of healing do believers provide, according to the following verses?

   a. Colossians 3:12–13

   b. 2 Corinthians 1:3–5

Topic C: Thirsty for God's Living Water

A key point of this session hinges on the imagery of water—the ice-cold water of Colosse, the warm water of Hierapolis, and the foul-tasting, lukewarm water of Laodicea. The imagery of water is used frequently in Scripture as it is in Revelation 3. As you study the following passages, consider the ways in which the world-famous water of Colosse is an image of what followers of Jesus have to offer to others.

PLANNING NOTES:

Topic C: Thirsty for God's Living Water

A key point of this session hinges on the imagery of water—the ice-cold water of Colosse, the warm water of Hierapolis, and the foul-tasting, luke-warm water of Laodicea. The imagery of water is used frequently in Scripture as it is in Revelation 3. As you study the following passages, consider the ways in which the world-famous water of Colosse is an image of what follow-ers of Jesus have to offer to others.

Waterfall of Colosse

1. David's psalms are known for their vivid descriptions of the human longing for God. Note the ways in which David expressed his desire for God in Psalm 42:1–2; 63:1. What do these descriptions tell us about our need for God?

   Suggested Responses: David com-pared his desire for God to that of a deer panting for water and the thirst of a person who lives in a parched land. Being thirsty for God is an incredible craving, an unrelenting desire to know Him better and have that spiritual need met.

   Note: All people are thirsty for God, but they may try to satisfy their thirst with other things instead.

2. What incredible, awesome promise does God make to spiritually thirsty people? (See Isaiah 41:17–18.)

   Suggested Responses: God will not forsake them! He will answer them and make "rivers flow on barren heights" and "turn the desert into pools of water." Consider how closely the waters of Colosse fit this description.

3. What was Jesus describing when He answered the Samaritan woman's ques-tion at the well? What was her response? (See John 4:10–15, also verses 16–42.)

   Suggested Responses: Using the image of water, Jesus described how anyone who received the "living water" that is God—the water that Jesus could give her—would be completely satisfied. Although she first wanted physical water, Jesus opened the woman's eyes to her spiritual need, and she apparently became a believer and testified to others, who became believers also.

3. What is the nature and source of the gift of healing, and why is it given? (See 1 Corinthians 12:7–12, 27–28.)

4. Read Matthew 25:31–46 and write down six types of healing in which believers are to be involved.

5. What other kinds of healing do believers provide, according to the following verses?

   a. Colossians 3:12–13

   b. 2 Corinthians 1:3–5

Topic C: Thirsty for God's Living Water

A key point of this session hinges on the imagery of water—the ice-cold water of Colosse, the warm water of Hierapolis, and the foul-tasting, lukewarm water of Laodicea. The imagery of water is used frequently in Scripture as it is in Revelation 3. As you study the following passages, consider the ways in which the world-famous water of Colosse is an image of what followers of Jesus have to offer to others.

1. David's psalms are known for their vivid descriptions of the human longing for God. Note the ways in which David expressed his desire for God in Psalm 42:1–2; 63:1. What do these descriptions tell us about our need for God?

Waterfall of Colosse

2. What incredible, awesome promise does God make to spiritually thirsty people? (See Isaiah 41:17–18.)

3. What was Jesus describing when He answered the Samaritan woman's question at the well? What was her response? (See John 4:10–15, also verses 16–42.)

✏ 4. What did Jesus promise to people in Jerusalem? (See John 7:37–39.)

Suggested Response: Jesus invited anyone who was spiritually thirsty to come to Him and drink, so that living water would spring up from within that person as well (which was a reference to the Holy Spirit whom believers would later receive).

✏ 5. According to Isaiah 32:1–2, what are righteous people—those who drink the living water of God—compared to and called to be?

Suggested Response: They become like a shelter from the wind, a refuge from a storm, streams of water flowing in the desert, and shade from the desert sun. In other words, godly people are to bring refreshment and relief to other people.

Topic D: Light and Darkness

To people in the ancient world, light and darkness held great meaning, so the Bible makes many references to light and darkness. Perhaps one reason the apostle John used the concept of "light" more than thirty times when writing to the church in Asia Minor is because the god Apollo was considered to be the god of music, prophecy, and light. Let's consider how the concept of light and darkness was used to communicate God's message to the people of Asia Minor.

✏ 1. To what was God compared in 2 Samuel 22:29?

Suggested Response: To a lamp that turns darkness into light.

✏ 2. What imagery did Isaiah use when he predicted the coming of the Messiah? (See Isaiah 9:2.)

Suggested Response: Isaiah referred to the Messiah as "a great light" that had dawned on people who walked in darkness and lived in the land of the shadow of death.

✏ 3. What did Paul urge the Ephesian Christians to do? (See Ephesians 5:8–14.)

Suggested Responses: Having once been "darkness," the Christians in Ephesus were to recognize that they had become "children of light" and had the fruit of goodness, righteousness, and truth. Thus he encouraged them to live as children of light and discover what pleases the Lord. They were also to flee the "fruitless deeds of darkness" and expose evil to the light of God.

✏ 4. As the Colossian Christians read Paul's letter, probably within sight of the Apollo temple of Hierapolis that adjoined the "Gates of Hades," what were they urged to do? (See Colossians 1:12–14.)

Suggested Responses: God had delivered them from the "dominion of darkness," from the evil in which they had lived. Having received salvation through their belief in Jesus, they were to thank God the Father for the inheritance they had in His kingdom—"the kingdom of light."

4. What did Jesus promise to people in Jerusalem? (See John 7:37–39.)

5. According to Isaiah 32:1–2, what are righteous people—those who drink the living water of God—compared to and called to be?

Topic D: Light and Darkness

To people in the ancient world, light and darkness held great meaning, so the Bible makes many references to light and darkness. Perhaps one reason the apostle John used the concept of "light" more than thirty times when writing to the church in Asia Minor is because the god Apollo was considered to be the god of music, prophecy, and light. Let's consider how the concept of light and darkness was used to communicate God's message to the people of Asia Minor.

1. To what was God compared in 2 Samuel 22:29?

2. What imagery did Isaiah use when he predicted the coming of the Messiah? (See Isaiah 9:2.)

3. What did Paul urge the Ephesian Christians to do? (See Ephesians 5:8–14.)

4. As the Colossian Christians read Paul's letter, probably within sight of the Apollo temple of Hierapolis that adjoined the "Gates of Hades," what were they urged to do? (See Colossians 1:12–14.)

5. Keeping in mind that Apollo was considered to be the god of light, yet was a counterfeit god who kept people in spiritual darkness, read John 8:12. How do you think followers of Apollo would have responded to what Jesus said about Himself?

6. What do you think it meant to the disciples when Jesus told them they were "the light of the world"? How might they have responded to followers of Apollo? (See Matthew 5:14–16.)

PLANNING NOTES:

5. Keeping in mind that Apollo was considered to be the god of light, yet was a counterfeit god who kept people in spiritual darkness, read John 8:12. How do you think followers of Apollo would have responded to what Jesus said about Himself?

Suggested Responses: No doubt devoted followers of Apollo would have been offended by this statement. Jesus claimed to be the light of the world, which is what their god claimed. Clearly Apollo or Jesus was a fake. Jesus offered quite a challenge when He said that anyone who followed Him would never walk in darkness.

6. What do you think it meant to the disciples when Jesus told them they were "the light of the world"? How might they have responded to followers of Apollo? (See Matthew 5:14–16.)

Suggested Responses: No doubt the disciples were proud to be identified with Jesus—the "light of the world." Jesus was saying that they, as His representatives, were true spiritual lights that could banish spiritual darkness, and if they let their light shine, people would praise God! These words would have encouraged them to shine even in the darkness of Apollo's evil.

DATA FILE

The Temple of Apollo in Hierapolis

Located on the main street between the theater and a sacred pool, this forty-by-sixty-foot temple was dedicated to the supposed god of light, Apollo. The entrance faced west and was approached by a broad flight of stairs.

Beneath the Temple of Apollo is the Plutonium, the cave that people believed led to the underworld. Pluto (or Hades, as the Greeks called him), was viewed as the god of the underworld and supposedly came and went via the opening to the cave, which was next to the temple.

The Plutonium played an important role in the culture of that day. Strabo, a Roman writer, described the fenced plaza in front of the cave opening where ceremonies took place. No doubt the consequences of entering the cave had much to do with its importance. All animals and most people, except the priests of the gods, died instantly if they entered it and breathed its poisonous gases. No one knows how the priests survived—perhaps they held their breath or had an unknown source of fresh air. Even today poisonous gases seep out of the cave, so its entrance is blocked by a fence to protect the unwary.

Apollo Temple

116   Faith Lessons on the Early Church

3. What did Paul urge the Ephesian Christians to do? (See Ephesians 5:8–14.)

4. As the Colossian Christians read Paul's letter, probably within sight of the Apollo temple of Hierapolis that adjoined the "Gates of Hades," what were they urged to do? (See Colossians 1:12–14.)

5. Keeping in mind that Apollo was considered to be the god of light, yet was a counterfeit god who kept people in spiritual darkness, read John 8:12. How do you think followers of Apollo would have responded to what Jesus said about Himself?

6. What do you think it meant to the disciples when Jesus told them they were "the light of the world"? How might they have responded to followers of Apollo? (See Matthew 5:14–16.)

Session Five: Hot or Cold   117

DATA FILE

The Temple of Apollo in Hierapolis

Located on the main street between the theater and a sacred pool, this forty-by-sixty-foot temple was dedicated to the supposed god of light, Apollo. The entrance faced west and was approached by a broad flight of stairs.

Beneath the Temple of Apollo is the Plutonium, the cave that people believed led to the underworld. Pluto (or Hades, as the Greeks called him), was viewed as the god of the underworld and supposedly came and went via the opening to the cave, which was next to the temple.

The Plutonium played an important role in the culture of that day. Strabo, a Roman writer, described the fenced plaza in front of the cave opening where ceremonies took place. No doubt the consequences of entering the cave had much to do with its importance. All animals and most people, except the priests of the gods, died instantly if they entered it and breathed its poisonous gases. No one knows how the priests survived—perhaps they held their breath or had an unknown source of fresh air. Even today poisonous gases seep out of the cave, so its entrance is blocked by a fence to protect the unwary.

Apollo Temple

Topic E: The Church in Colosse

Although the city of Colosse was in decline, this city of cold, fresh, rushing water had a vibrant Christian community.

1. Who founded the church in Colosse? (See Acts 19:8–10; Colossians 1:1–7.)

   Suggested Responses: Epaphras did, but Paul's teaching had spread to the city as well.

2. How well did Paul know the Colossian believers? (See Colossians 1:3–4.)

   Suggested Response: Paul had heard a great deal about their faith but had never visited them.

3. The brief letter of Philemon is addressed to one of the leaders of the church in Colosse. Note what it reveals about the believers there.

   a. What had Paul heard about them and what impact did it have on him? (See Philemon 1–7.)

   Suggested Responses: He had heard about their faith and their love. Their love gave him "joy and encouragement" and "refreshed the hearts of the saints!" How amazing that the church in the city of refreshing water refreshed others.

   b. What did Paul ask the Colossians to do? (See Philemon 6.)

   Suggested Response: Paul asked the believers there to actively share their faith so that their knowledge of Christ would be complete.

   c. What did Paul specifically ask Philemon to do, and what did he expect would be the outcome? (See Philemon 10–22.)

   Suggested Responses: He asked Philemon to welcome Onesimus as a brother (Onesimus was Philemon's former slave who had run away after stealing some money and then become a Christian), and to prepare a guest room for Paul in case he could visit them. Paul's respect for Philemon and his confidence that he would do the right thing is evident.

4. According to Colossians 2:8, 16–21, which challenges was the church facing?

   Suggested Responses: Some believers were being led astray by "hollow and deceptive philosophy"; unbelievers were judging the Christians by what they ate, drank, and how they celebrated religious festivals or Sabbath days; people with false humility who had lost touch with Jesus—the "Head" of the body of Christ—were preaching about angel worship; and believers were following unnecessary, legalistic rules.

   > Signal the groups when one minute remains so that they may wrap up their discovery time.

Topic E: The Church in Colosse

Although the city of Colosse was in decline, this city of cold, fresh, rushing water had a vibrant Christian community.

1. Who founded the church in Colosse? (See Acts 19:8–10; Colossians 1:1–7)

2. How well did Paul know the Colossian believers? (See Colossians 1:3–4.)

3. The brief letter of Philemon is addressed to one of the leaders of the church in Colosse. Note what it reveals about the believers there.

   a. What had Paul heard about them and what impact did it have on him? (See Philemon 1–7.)

   b. What did Paul ask the Colossians to do? (See Philemon 6.)

   c. What did Paul specifically ask Philemon to do, and what did he expect would be the outcome? (See Philemon 10–22.)

4. According to Colossians 2:8, 16–21, which challenges was the church facing?

DATA FILE

Laodicea

History

The leading city in the valley during the first century, Laodicea was destroyed by an earthquake in A.D. 60. According to Roman writer Tacitus, Rome offered to pay for the city to be rebuilt, but the people declined, saying that they were wealthy enough to restore their own city.

Industry

The city was renowned for three main industries:

- a banking center for the province of Asia Minor, including a gold exchange;
- the textile center where glossy, black wool was woven into garments called *trimata* that were prized in the Roman world;
- the location of a major medical school known worldwide and where an eye salve called Phyrigian powder was made from a local stone.

Encrusted Stone Water Pipes of Laodicea

Geography

Located in the fertile Lycus River Valley, the city had no nearby water source, so tepid, mineral-filled, and nauseating water was piped in from six miles away.

DATA FILE
Laodicea

History

The leading city in the valley during the first century, Laodicea was destroyed by an earthquake in A.D. 60. According to Roman writer Tacitus, Rome offered to pay for the city to be rebuilt, but the people declined, saying that they were wealthy enough to restore their own city.

Industry

The city was renowned for three main industries:

- a banking center for the province of Asia Minor, including a gold exchange;
- the textile center where glossy, black wool was woven into garments called *trimata* that were prized in the Roman world;
- the location of a major medical school known worldwide and where an eye salve called Phyrigian powder was made from a local stone.

Geography

Located in the fertile Lycus River Valley, the city had no nearby water source, so tepid, mineral-filled, and nauseating water was piped in from six miles away.

Encrusted Stone Water Pipes of Laodicea

DID YOU KNOW?

What Happened to the Church in Laodicea?

Church history records that the church in Laodicea remained dynamic after most churches in Asia disappeared. One of its bishops was martyred for his faith in A.D. 161, about seventy years after John wrote his warning to the city in the book of Revelation. In A.D. 363, Laodicea was the location chosen for a significant church council. So, it appears that the church in Laodicea learned its lesson and God continued to bless the Christian community there for some time.

4. According to Colossians 2:8, 16–21, which challenges was the church facing?

DATA FILE

Laodicea

History

The leading city in the valley during the first century, Laodicea was destroyed by an earthquake in A.D. 60. According to Roman writer Tacitus, Rome offered to pay for the city to be rebuilt, but the people declined, saying that they were wealthy enough to restore their own city.

Industry

The city was renowned for three main industries:

- a banking center for the province of Asia Minor, including a gold exchange;
- the textile center where glossy, black wool was woven into garments called *trimata* that were prized in the Roman world;
- the location of a major medical school known worldwide and where an eye salve called Phyrigian powder was made from a local stone.

Encrusted Stone Water Pipes of Laodicea

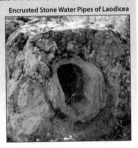

Geography

Located in the fertile Lycus River Valley, the city had no nearby water source, so tepid, mineral-filled, and nauseating water was piped in from six miles away.

DID YOU KNOW?

What Happened to the Church in Laodicea?

Church history records that the church in Laodicea remained dynamic after most churches in Asia disappeared. One of its bishops was martyred for his faith in A.D. 161, about seventy years after John wrote his warning to the city in the book of Revelation. In A.D. 363, Laodicea was the location chosen for a significant church council. So, it appears that the church in Laodicea learned its lesson and God continued to bless the Christian community there for some time.

faith lesson

Time for Reflection

Read the following passage of Scripture and take the next few minutes to consider what this passage may have meant to the believers in Laodicea and what it means for Christians today.

"To the angel of the church in Laodicea write:

These are the words of the Amen, the faithful and true witness, the ruler of God's creation. I know your deeds, that you are neither cold nor hot. I wish you were either one or the other! So, because you are lukewarm—neither hot nor cold—I am about to spit you out of my mouth. You say, 'I am rich; I have acquired wealth and do not need a thing.' But you do not realize that you are wretched, pitiful, poor, blind and naked. I counsel you to buy from me gold refined in the fire, so you can become rich; and white clothes to wear, so you can cover your shameful nakedness; and salve to put on your eyes, so you can see.

Those whom I love I rebuke and discipline. So be earnest, and repent.

Revelation 3:14–19

PLANNING NOTES:

faith lesson

Time for Reflection (5 minutes)

It's time for each of us to think quietly about how we can apply what we've learned today. On page 120 of the Participant's Guide, you'll find a passage of Scripture. Let's each read this passage silently and take the next few minutes to consider what this passage may have meant to the believers in Laodicea and what it means for Christians today.

Please do not talk during this time. It's a time when we all can reflect on today's lesson and how it applies to our lives.

> The Scripture passage and questions are reproduced in their entirety in the Participant's Guide on pages 120–22.

"To the angel of the church in Laodicea write:

These are the words of the Amen, the faithful and true witness, the ruler of God's creation. I know your deeds, that you are neither cold nor hot. I wish you were either one or the other! So, because you are lukewarm—neither hot nor cold—I am about to spit you out of my mouth. You say, 'I am rich; I have acquired wealth and do not need a thing.' But you do not realize that you are wretched, pitiful, poor, blind and naked. I counsel you to buy from me gold refined in the fire, so you can become rich; and white clothes to wear, so you can cover your shameful nakedness; and salve to put on your eyes, so you can see.

Those whom I love I rebuke and discipline. So be earnest, and repent. (Revelation 3:14–19)

God's inspired Word speaks to all people. Although a person can understand the Bible without knowing the cultural settings in which particular books were written, one can learn even more by learning the common images and symbols the biblical writers used. The apostle John used a number of metaphors from history, culture, and geography in his Revelation 3 letter to the church in Laodicea. Based on what you've learned in this session, consider what these metaphors meant to the people and what they mean to you today:

Phrase Used	What This Phrase May Have Referred to
You are neither cold	*The refreshingly cold, thirst-quenching, mountain-fed water of Colosse.*
…nor hot	*The warm, healing, soothing water of the Hierapolis hot springs.*
Because you are lukewarm	*The water of Laodicea, which was tepid and disgusting and was carried by stone pipes from six miles away.*
I am about to spit you out of my mouth	*The water of Laodicea was so bad that people could hardly drink it and quite likely spit it out.*
You say, "I am rich; I have acquired wealth and do not need a thing"	*After an earthquake destroyed Laodicea in A.D. 60, the Roman emperor offered to rebuild the city, but the people refused, saying they had enough money to do it themselves.*

(chart continued on page 194)

DID YOU KNOW?

What Happened to the Church in Laodicea?
Church history records that the church in Laodicea remained dynamic after most churches in Asia disappeared. One of its bishops was martyred for his faith in A.D. 161, about seventy years after John wrote his warning to the city in the book of Revelation. In A.D. 363, Laodicea was the location chosen for a significant church council. So, it appears that the church in Laodicea learned its lesson and God continued to bless the Christian community there for some time.

faith Lesson

Time for Reflection

Read the following passage of Scripture and take the next few minutes to consider what this passage may have meant to the believers in Laodicea and what it means for Christians today.

"To the angel of the church in Laodicea write:

These are the words of the Amen, the faithful and true witness, the ruler of God's creation. I know your deeds, that you are neither cold nor hot. I wish you were either one or the other! So, because you are lukewarm—neither hot nor cold—I am about to spit you out of my mouth. You say, 'I am rich; I have acquired wealth and do not need a thing.' But you do not realize that you are wretched, pitiful, poor, blind and naked. I counsel you to buy from me gold refined in the fire, so you can become rich; and white clothes to wear, so you can cover your shameful nakedness; and salve to put on your eyes, so you can see.

Those whom I love I rebuke and discipline. So be earnest, and repent.

REVELATION 3:14–19

God's inspired Word speaks to all people. Although a person can understand the Bible without knowing the cultural settings in which particular books were written, one can learn even more by learning the common images and symbols the biblical writers used. The apostle John used a number of metaphors from history, culture, and geography in his Revelation 3 letter to the church in Laodicea. Based on what you've learned in this session, consider what these metaphors meant to the people and what they mean to you today:

Phrase Used	What This Phrase May Have Referred To
You are neither cold	
. . . nor hot	
Because you are lukewarm	
I am about to spit you out of my mouth	
You say, "I am rich; I have acquired wealth and do not need a thing"	
But you do not realize you are wretched, pitiful, poor, blind and naked	
I counsel you to buy from me gold refined in the fire	
White clothes to wear	
Salve to put on your eyes, so you can see	

PLANNING NOTES:

(continued from page 192)

But you do not realize you are wretched, pitiful, poor, blind and naked	*These were powerful words for people who lived in an extremely wealthy, powerful city that was known for its medical school, the eye salve that helped people's eyesight, and its black-wool clothing. (See Matthew 13:13–15; 2 Corinthians 4:4.)*
I counsel you to buy from me gold refined in the fire	*In Laodicea, a key banking center, merchants commonly handled gold-related transactions and currency exchanges. (See 1 Corinthians 3:10–15; 1 Peter 1:6–7.)*
White clothes to wear	*This established a contrast between the white clothing John mentioned and the black wool clothing for which the city was famous throughout the Roman world.*
Salve to put on your eyes, so you can see	*John really made a point here, since the city was known for its Phyrigian powder, an eye salve that was shipped around the world.*

If you were to describe a type of water to symbolize your walk with God right now, consider the kind of water you would choose. Would it be stagnant? A fast-flowing mountain stream? A clear, sparkling pool? A warm bath? A thundering waterfall?

Action Points (4 minutes)

The following points are reproduced on pages 122–24 of the Participant's Guide:

Now it's time to wrap up our session.

Give participants a moment to transition from their thoughtfulness to giving you their full attention.

I'd like to take a moment to summarize the key points we explored. After I have reviewed these points, I will give you a moment to jot down an action step (or steps) that you will commit to this week as a result of what you have learned today.

Read the following points and pause afterward so that participants can consider and write out their commitment.

1. *John, when writing to the church in Laodicea, used images of the Laodiceans' everyday world in order to communicate God's message.* He referred to what the Laodiceans had told the Roman emperor who wanted to help them rebuild their city. He mentioned blindness to a city whose key industry was making and marketing eye salve. And he described their faith in terms of the local water—the most basic necessity of life.

    Which commonly understood images of culture are you able to use in communicating God's message to spiritually needy people?

God's inspired Word speaks to all people. Although a person can understand the Bible without knowing the cultural settings in which particular books were written, one can learn even more by learning the common images and symbols the biblical writers used. The apostle John used a number of metaphors from history, culture, and geography in his Revelation 3 letter to the church in Laodicea. Based on what you've learned in this session, consider what these metaphors meant to the people and what they mean to you today:

Phrase Used	What This Phrase May Have Referred To
You are neither cold	
…nor hot	
Because you are lukewarm	
I am about to spit you out of my mouth	
You say, "I am rich; I have acquired wealth and do not need a thing"	
But you do not realize you are wretched, pitiful, poor, blind and naked	
I counsel you to buy from me gold refined in the fire	
White clothes to wear	
Salve to put on your eyes, so you can see	

If you were to describe a type of water to symbolize your walk with God right now, consider the kind of water you would choose. Would it be stagnant? A fast-flowing mountain stream? A clear, sparkling pool? A warm bath? A thundering waterfall?

Action Points

Take a moment to jot down an action step (or steps) that you will commit to this week as a result of what you have learned.

1. *John, when writing to the church in Laodicea, used images of the Laodiceans' everyday world in order to communicate God's message.* He referred to what the Laodiceans had told the Roman emperor who wanted to help them rebuild their city. He mentioned blindness to a city whose key industry was making and marketing eye salve. And he described their faith in terms of the local water—the most basic necessity of life.

   Which commonly understood images of culture are you able to use in communicating God's message to spiritually needy people?

   In what specific ways might you use your background, training, and/or interests to better communicate the message of Jesus to your world?

In what specific ways might you use your background, training, and/or interests to better communicate the message of Jesus to your world?

2. *God longs for those who follow Him to be wholehearted and passionate in offering His message to a hurting world.* Like the water of Colosse, which was cold, fresh, and invigorating, followers of Christ offer a message that is refreshing to hearts that are weary of sin. Like the warm, healing mineral waters of Hierapolis, followers of Christ offer a message that brings healing to those who are wounded and broken by sin. And like the nauseating, tepid water of Laodicea, followers who do nothing, who are neither hot nor cold, turn God's stomach.

What's your temperature?

In which practical ways can you be more like hot water, bringing healing and comfort to hurting people? To whom?

In which ways can you be more like cold water, sharing encouragement through the empowering, caring love of Jesus the Messiah? To whom?

3. *Using what Jesus had taught them, or what they had learned through other believers, early Christians such as Philip passionately proclaimed the gospel throughout the Roman world. Consequently, God used them to change that world!* Christians today have no less of an opportunity to live as Jesus' disciples and bring His message to a lost and hurting world.

Do you believe that God can use you to change your world?

Identify some aspect of your faith—your knowledge of God's Word, your walk with God—that you can be passionate about sharing with others. Ask God to help you to be more faithful and bold in sharing this truth with your world.

closing prayer
I minute

Dear God, this session on Laodicea has reminded us of how important it is to live as Your talmidim—to love You passionately, to follow You wholeheartedly, to know You and seek to be like You, and to demonstrate Your love to people around us. Please help us share Your light with people who live in spiritual darkness, to become more sensitive to the opportunities You place before us to bring Your healing and restoring love to hurting people. Fill us with Your Spirit so we can refresh other people because of what You have given us. Help us to be Your loving hands to people in need. In Your name we pray. Amen.

2. *God longs for those who follow Him to be wholehearted and passionate in offering His message to a hurting world.* Like the water of Colosse, which was cold, fresh, and invigorating, followers of Christ offer a message that is refreshing to hearts that are weary of sin. Like the warm, healing mineral waters of Hierapolis, followers of Christ offer a message that brings healing to those who are wounded and broken by sin. And like the nauseating, tepid water of Laodicea, followers who do nothing, who are neither hot nor cold, turn God's stomach.

What's your temperature?

In which practical ways can you be more like hot water, bringing healing and comfort to hurting people? To whom?

In which ways can you be more like cold water, sharing encouragement through the empowering, caring love of Jesus the Messiah? To whom?

3. *Using what Jesus had taught them, or what they had learned through other believers, early Christians such as Philip passionately proclaimed the gospel throughout the Roman world. Consequently, God used them to change that world!* Christians today have no less of an opportunity to

live as Jesus' disciples and bring His message to a lost and hurting world.

Do you believe that God can use you to change your world?

Identify some aspect of your faith—your knowledge of God's Word, your walk with God—that you can be passionate about sharing with others. Ask God to help you to be more faithful and bold in sharing this truth with your world.

PLANNING NOTES:

additional resources

To learn more about the cultural and geographical background of the Bible, consult the following resources:

Akurgal, Ekrem. *Ancient Civilizations and Ruins of Turkey.* Istanbul: Haset Kitabevi, 1985.

Beitzel, Barry J. *Moody Bible Atlas of Bible Lands.* Chicago: Moody Press, 1993.

Bivin, David. *Understanding the Difficult Words of Jesus.* Shippensburg, PA: Destiny Image Publishers, 1994.

Butler, Trent C., ed. *Holman Bible Dictionary.* Nashville: Holman Bible Publishers, 1991.

Crawford, John S. "Multiculturalism at Sardis." *Biblical Archaeology Review* (Sept.–Oct. 1996).

De Vries, LaMoine F. *Cities of the Biblical World.* Peabody, MA: Hendrikson, 1997.

Edmonds, Anna G. *Turkey's Religious Sites.* Istanbul: Damko, 1997.

Friesen, Steven. "Ephesus: Key to a Vision in Revelation," *Biblical Archaeological Review* (May–June 1993).

Hamilton, Edith. *Mythology.* New York: Penguin Books, 1969.

Safrai, Shmuel, M. Stern, D. Flusser, and W. C. Van Unnik. *The Jewish People in the First Century.* 9 vols. Amsterdam: Van Gorcum, 1974.

Visalli, Gayla. *After Jesus: The Triumph of Christianity.* New York: Reader's Digest, 1992.

Ward, Kaari. *Jesus and His Times.* New York: Reader's Digest, 1987.

Yamauchi, Edwin. *The Archaeology of New Testament Cities in Western Asia Minor.* Grand Rapids: Baker Book House, 1980.

Young, Brad. *Jesus the Jewish Theologian.* Peabody, MA: Hendrikson, 1995.

———. *Paul the Jewish Theologian.* Peabody, MA: Hendrikson, 1999.

transform your life through a journey of discovery into the world of the Bible

Faith Lessons Video Series

Filmed on location in Israel, **Faith Lessons** is a unique video series that brings God's Word to life with astounding relevance. By weaving together the Bible's fascinating historical, cultural, religious, and geographical contexts, teacher and historian Ray Vander Laan reveals keen insights into Scripture's significance for modern believers. These illuminating "faith lessons" afford a new understanding of the Bible that will ground your convictions and transform your life.

The **Faith Lessons** video series is ideal for use at home, especially in personal and family Bible studies. Individual believers and families will gain vital insights from long-ago times and cultures through this innovative approach to Bible study.

"Nothing has opened and illuminated the Scriptures for me quite like the Faith Lessons series."

—Dr. James Dobson

**Faith Lessons on
the Promised Land**
Crossroads of the World
Volume One
0-310-67864-1

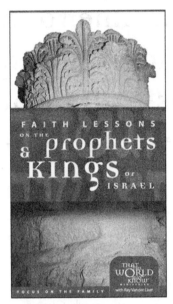

**Faith Lessons on
the Prophets &
Kings of Israel
Volume Two**
0-310-67865-X

**Faith Lessons on
the Life & Ministry
of the Messiah
Volume Three**
0-310-67866-8

**Faith Lessons on the
Death & Resurrection
of the Messiah
Volume Four**
0-310-67867-6

**Faith Lessons on
the Early Church
Volume Five**
0-310-67962-1

Travel back in time to see the sights, hear the sounds, and experience the wonder of Jesus—all through the power of interactive CD-ROM.

Jesus
An Interactive Journey

Imagine traveling back in time for a life-changing encounter with Christ . . . meeting the people who knew Him . . . retracing His footsteps . . . seeing firsthand what His life was like.

Now, through the cutting-edge technology of interactive CD-ROM, you can make that incredible voyage—back to the life and times of Jesus! This exciting multimedia adventure takes you there, giving you an entirely new appreciation for the fascinating historical, geographical, and cultural backdrop that will enhance your understanding of the Gospel.

An innovative "Visitor's Center" is your gateway to more than 180 different avenues of study, from Christ's birth to His resurrection. With a click of the mouse, you'll be guided to dozens of colorful locales, where you'll experience through the eyes and ears of ancient Jews and Romans what Christ's world was really like.

Or take a self-guided tour and stroll at your own pace through the lively marketplace to learn about trade and commerce, pause to listen in on the people, or go to the synagogue to gain a better understanding of the religious practices of the day.

Compatible with Windows® 95 and Windows® 3.1

0-310-67888-9

We want to hear from you. Please send your comments about
this book to us in care of the address below. Thank you.

ZondervanPublishingHouse
Grand Rapids, Michigan 49530
http://www.zondervan.com